**Bun Hashizume:**

Poet, writer and atom[...] was fourteen and only 1.[...] when the atomic bomb was dropped on Hiroshima, seriously injuring her. In 1985, her first anthology of 'atomic bomb' poetry titled *The Youth Who Turned into an Insect* appeared. Other poetry collections include *Like an Abandoned Swing* (1990) and *Returning to the Earth; Rising to the Heavens* (2009). Many of her 'atomic bomb' poems have been set to music and performed in concerts in Japan and overseas. Essay collections and memoirs include *Turkey – A Mysterious and Wonderful Land* (1993), *Memoirs of the Atomic Bomb: The Experiences of a Fourteen-Year-Old Girl* (2001), and *From Hiroshima* (2014). Currently residing in Tokyo, Hashizume continues to write and give talks nationwide, and occasionally overseas.

**Image of Bun at around 18 years old (1949). Taken inside the Atomic Bomb Dome where graffiti is clearly visible on the inner walls – today it is no longer possible to enter the Dome.**
**Bun is wearing a suit that she hand made from a woolen blanket distributed with the relief supplies after the bombing, and a white jabot (neck ruffle) made from fabric scraps.**

**Susan Bouterey:**

Susan Bouterey (DPhil, Tokyo University) is a Senior Lecturer in the Department of Global, Cultural and Language Studies, University of Canterbury, New Zealand. Key areas of research are contemporary Japanese literature including Japanese women writers' fiction, atomic bomb literature, and Okinawan fiction. She also specializes in literary translation and has translated a number of Hashizume's works to date. Monographs include *Medoruma Shun's World: History, Memory, Narrative* (2011). Literary translations include *Water's Edge* by Tsushima Yūko in *More Stories by Japanese Women Writers* (2011), *Fellow Humans! Let Us Foster Love & Wisdom – From Hiroshima* (1997), *Living Together* and *Little Brother* in *Australian Multicultural Book Review* (1996).

This book is dedicated to the children of the world and future generations.

Bun Hashizume
Translated By: Susan Bouterey

# THE DAY THE SUN FELL

## MEMOIRS OF A SURVIVOR OF THE ATOMIC BOMB

AUSTIN MACAULEY PUBLISHERS™

LONDON • CAMBRIDGE • NEW YORK • SHARJAH

A CIP catalogue record for this title is available from the British Library.

ISBN 9781788780889 (Paperback)
ISBN 9781788780896 (Hardback)
ISBN 9781528955096 (ePub e-book)

www.austinmacauley.com

First Published (2019)
Austin Macauley Publishers Ltd
25 Canada Square
Canary Wharf
London
E14 5LQ

It is through the untiring efforts of Watanabe Tomoko, the Executive Director of ANT-Hiroshima, an NGO that pursues projects in international cooperation, international peace-building, and peace education, that I have been able to record these events for posterity. I express my immense gratitude to her for publishing the original Japanese version of this book.

If my encounter with Watanabe Tomoko was a meeting of like minds, I had an even more miraculous encounter with her mother. On August 6<sup>th</sup>, 1945, as Hiroshima city was consumed in flames, we lay on either side of the same bush in the gardens of the Red Cross Hospital – a fact that I only discovered in the midst of the Fukushima disaster by which time we were eighty-one and eighty respectively. We are now like sisters, addressing each other with the familiar terms 'Teru-chan' and 'Fumi-chan'.

An earlier version of this book was published as *Shōjo, Jūyonsai no Genbaku Taiken-ki* (*Record of a Fourteen-Year-Old Girl's Experiences of the Atomic Bomb*) in 2001 by Kōbunken and immediately translated into French by Pierre Regnier. Elizabeth Leeper, the partner of Steven Leeper, former President of the Hiroshima Peace Culture Foundation, spent much time with atomic-bomb survivors when she was in Hiroshima. When she discovered this book, she exclaimed, "This is just the work that I had been looking for!" and started working on translating it into English. However, she had to return to America in order to look after her parents and was unable to get any further than the first chapter.

The current book is the result of extensive revisions and additions to *Record of a Fourteen-Year-Old Girl's Experiences of the Atomic Bomb*. I am indebted to Kikkawa Hikaru for his helpful comments and editing of my work in the original, and for dispatching each and every chapter to Susan Bouterey for translating.

Susan and my friendship goes back more than twenty years. Whenever I visit New Zealand, she welcomes me like family into her home and on my solo travels around the world to spread the anti-nuclear message, I always take along copies of a booklet containing her translations of my essay and poems on my atomic-bomb experiences. These I distribute, sowing 'anti-nuclear seeds' that have now taken root in many places across the globe.

Susan likewise wishes to acknowledge the generous assistance of Mr Kikkawa. Additionally, she expresses her deep gratitude to friends and family for their unwavering support and encouragement. Without this, and their invaluable comments on the translation, this translation may not have materialized.

Susan and I would also like to acknowledge the generous grant in support of the publication made by the School of Language, Social and Political Sciences, College of Arts, University of Canterbury.

Finally, we would like to express our gratitude to the production team and editors at Austin Macauley. We are grateful to Rebecca Ponting, who welcomed us to Austin Macauley in the first instance; and to Harry Robinson for his patience, efficiency, and professionalism in bringing this publishing project to fruition.

# Table of Contents

# Preface

This book of memoirs is in the form of a loose collection of essays, many on Hiroshima – especially my experience of the atomic bombing of the city – and the people living in Hiroshima at the time of the blast, some on my solo travels overseas from my late sixties, and others that capture events from the time of the Fukushima Nuclear Power Plant disaster in March 2011 through to the present day. People who have read my memoirs pass comment that they are 'not gloomy', 'quite unlike most memoirs on the blast'. I wonder why that is? The horror of the atomic bombing can never be fully captured in the written or spoken word. Neither do I have the power to fully express in writing the painful struggles I have faced over the years as I endured illnesses and other hardships. Or perhaps it is the case that something transcending immense suffering, beyond reason – a sad acceptance and compassion for all things – has been cultivated in me.

Hashizume Bun

# The Day the Sun Fell

On the morning of August 6, 1945, I stepped outside and looked up at another serene blue Hiroshima sky. The air raid siren had shattered the air earlier but they'd soon given the all clear. Had it been a false alarm?[1] The cicadas in the garden cedars were awake and chirping loudly; it promised to be another hot day.

I was fourteen, in my third year at girls' college, and had been assigned under the student mobilization scheme[2] to work in the Savings Bureau of the Department of Communications. My family lived in a northern district of the city, near Hiroshima Castle, while the Savings Bureau was situated in the south of the city, close to the Red Cross Hospital. Consequently, I spent an hour each morning traversing the city on foot to get to work as students were forbidden from travelling on the trams at the time. Life was such that people typically walked distances of two to three kilometers.

When the air raid siren went off that morning, I had been en route to work. I returned home briefly then headed out again, arriving at work just after 8 am, some thirty or so minutes late. As usual, I slipped through the side entrance and climbed the narrow back staircase to the office on the third floor. The Savings Bureau was in a box-shaped, four-story building made of ferroconcrete. I vaguely recall that the ground floor was the customer service section, providing postal services and the like.

---

[1] The Japanese radar operators were apparently deceived by the small number of planes; detecting only three, they assumed they were doing a reconnaissance and gave the 'all clear'.

[2] There was a severe labor shortage in Japan at the time, as all the healthy young men had been drafted into the army. Women and students were required, therefore, to work in their place.

Administrative work was conducted on the upper floors, with each of the floors from the second upwards named Savings Division Two, Three, and Four respectively. I was assigned to Savings Division Three on the third floor. My close friends were working in Savings Division Four.

Each floor, with the exception I imagine of the ground floor, featured a large open office area with a mezzanine floor in one corner. The mezzanine floor held a vault for keeping the ledgers, sturdily built to ensure these valuable documents were securely housed. Inside the vault, the walls were lined with floor-to-ceiling shelving stacked with ledgers neatly ordered by customer name. There was barely enough space between the crammed shelves for two people to squeeze past.

On arrival at work, our first task as student workers was to collect the bundles of savings slips, delivered the previous day from savings banks across the city, and take them upstairs to the vault on the mezzanine floor. There we would pull out the appropriate ledgers as we checked them against the customers' names on the slips. At the end of the day, our final task would be to return the processed ledgers to their rightful place. In between these tasks, we filled in the hours by performing odd jobs and practicing writing Arabic numerals in the Communication Bureau's distinctive style.

Once a month, Savings Bureau staff would gather for an abacus competition. Ms. Tomoyanagi, a female worker in the same division as me, would win hands down every time, without fail. Ms. Tomoyanagi was a placid, remarkably down-to-earth person. I'm not sure exactly how it came about but eventually, at lunch break and whenever else there was free time, I could be found avidly practicing the abacus under her tutelage. And it was Ms. Tomoyanagi who saved my life on the day of the blast.

When the bomb exploded, my girlfriends were in the vault with the ledgers on the fourth floor – they lived on the southern side of the city so they had probably been able to get to work earlier than me. This apparently saved them.

The previous day, the Savings Bureau had distributed canned mandarin oranges to each of the mobilized students. One of the many 'luxury goods' at the time, canned mandarins were hard to come by, like gold. Mother put my can safely away in the cupboard, planning to take it on her next visit to see my younger brother and sister who were staying in a temple in the countryside where they had been evacuated with their classmates.

On arrival at work, I went directly to see the section head with payment for the can of mandarins. His desk was next to the window, facing inward. I had just approached him and was holding out the money when I saw a tremendous flash of light through the window behind him. It came from the northwest district, causing me to momentarily turn my eyes in that direction; they were met by a dazzlingly beautiful rainbow streaming with hundreds and thousands of brilliantly colored rays of light.

For a brief moment I thought that the sun had fallen, that heaven and earth had switched places...

I must have passed out. When I came to, I found myself squatting in a cramped, pitch-black space. Thinking I had been blinded, I tried to get into the air-raid posture that that had been drilled into us daily – middle and forefingers pressed against the eyes to prevent the eyeballs from popping out, thumbs against the ears to stop the eardrums from shattering, belly against the floor to prevent abdominal injuries – but there seemed to be no room to manoeuver. I stayed in a squat, fingers pressed tightly against my eyes and ears, my body tense and alert. An eerie silence hung over the room. Presently, I felt something warm and sticky running down my right arm. I wondered if a napalm bomb[3] had hit our building and it was the oil trickling down from the floor above. If so, it would be a sea of flames up there. I imagined my classmates darting about the large office, desperately trying to escape the flames. Worried, I scrunched into an even tighter ball.

The warm sticky trickle down my arm was now a steady stream. I cautiously removed my hands from my eyes and ears. The darkness shifted so that I could vaguely make things out. I

---

[3] A particularly lethal type of incendiary bomb that consists of petroleum, or some other such fuel, mixed with a gelling agent to create an extremely sticky and inflammable substance. Developed in World War II, napalm was used extensively in US air attacks on Japanese cities during the war.

slowly stretched my hands out in front of me, only to discover that my palms were covered in blood. It seemed I had suffered an injury to the head, somewhere above my right ear. Remembering the first-aid kit in my desk, I scrambled to my feet, then reeled at the sight that met my eyes; clouds of dust filled the room and, across the floor, desks, chairs and bookshelves lay upturned and on end, in a crumpled heap. I appeared to be standing next to one of the central pillars; the blast must have thrown me halfway across the room. *Where on earth was my desk?* I clambered over the rubble of desks and chairs and pushed them aside until I eventually located it. Whipping out a large bandage from my first-aid kit, I had just tied it around my head when I heard a hoarse shout, "Out, everyone!" One after another dark figures emerged from the sooty black clouds of dust and smoke, and staggered toward the exit.

A high-voltage power line ran past our window on the third floor. Broken by the blast, it had sprung into our office and now lay in a large heap on the floor, its coils winding almost to the ceiling at the southern end of the room. My desk was in the northeast corner of the room, on the far side of the exit. I approached the electric wires and gingerly reached out to touch one. It was dead. With my right hand pressed against the wound to my head, and using my other hand to push away the coils, I gradually worked my way across the room. Progress was slow as my legs kept getting caught up in the wire. I tripped many times before coming to an abrupt halt. At my feet, lying face up, entangled in the wires, was one of the office workers, a chap we fondly called Chiang Kai-shek on account of his shaven head and similar features to the former Chinese Nationalist Party leader. His pale, waxen face showed no sign of any injury but he was dead. I turned cold with fear. This was my first encounter with death that day.

I managed to make it out to the corridor where I found colleagues from the third floor and those descending from the fourth floor. They looked like a parade of ghosts as, with wildly disheveled hair and sooty bodies, they jostled to get to the staircase. I joined the throng but had descended no more than two or three steps when I stumbled into a little girl collapsed naked on the steps in front of me. The blast must have ripped off her clothing. Pale pink intestines bulged from a gash to her abdomen. It was the cleaner's daughter, a four or five-year old called Yuki-chan, as I recall. Yuki-chan used to come to our office with her mother and, duster or broom in hand, pretend she was helping. She was a friendly, adorable little girl, with peaches and cream skin and large round eyes. The women and girls in the office especially doted on her, painting her face up like a doll, with white powder and red lipstick, both luxuries at the time. Now the child lay naked and writhing in agony. Every time she moved more of her intestines spilled out, piling up by her stomach before my very eyes. One of my friends told me that she later saw the girl's mother standing shaken and badly injured on the landing at the top of the stairs cradling her wounded daughter in her arms, and imploring people to save her child.

With barely enough room on the narrow staircase to make way for anyone, people were simply stepping over Yuki-chan as they fled. I had stopped at the sight of her but was soon pushed forward by the crowd behind me. I chanted a Buddhist sutra as I too was forced to step over her. Invoking Buddha's name at that moment gave me occasion later to reflect on my religious views. I was the eldest daughter[4] of an eldest son, raised in a strongly patriarchal age. Perhaps to get me out from under the bustling feet of the adults when I was little, my grandmother often took me along with her to hear Buddhist sermons at the local temple. Grandmother said the priest at the temple, whom everyone called Goinge-san, was highly ranked because he donned red silk and purple robes.

The purpose of the sermons was to help people attain the Pure Land of Paradise upon their death, and all those who came to listen would head home with a look of heartfelt piety and the Buddhist chant, '*namu amida-butsu*', on their lips. Even as a toddler, I was able to understand the sermons; my mother said that I had been precocious, already running around before my first birthday, and quick at picking things up. At first, I would sit there quietly listening to the sermons, but it wasn't long before I grew bored and wandered out to peer at the scroll

---

[4] Bun has an older sister, but she is a half-sister from a different father so Bun is the oldest daughter in the Kaneyuki family.

paintings in the main passageway circling the hall. The paintings depicted the paradise and hell that the priest, Goingesan, spoke of. They raised endless questions in my mind as a child: *Is this really true? Has anyone ever seen these places and come back? Is there really another world after death?*

The adults' words and actions only served to fuel my doubts. From what I could see, they were the picture of virtue when listening to the sermons, but once they were back home and going about their everyday lives, they would be speaking ill of others and telling lies. *Are all these people headed for hell?* I wondered. This is how I learned of human duplicity and developed a mysterious fascination in Buddha and people's belief in the religion. When I caught myself chanting a Buddhist sutra as I stepped over Yuki-chan, I determined to give some more thought to the matter of religion.

Not long after the end of the war, missionaries and nuns arrived on Hiroshima's scorched plains preaching Christianity. Even though it was a struggle simply to survive, I would attend bible readings in the evenings and go out during lunch breaks at work to listen to lectures by nuns in the neighborhood. So enthusiastic was I, they would encourage me to become baptized. Years later, when I was married and living in Kamakura, early mornings would find me in a Zen temple. In the end, however, I was not to be won over by either religion.

The narrow staircase was jam-packed with people desperately trying to flee. Progress was slow. As I inched my way down the stairs, I caught sight of the city through a window on the landing. *What on earth can be happening?* I thought, as the houses on the left began collapsing like dominoes, followed shortly by the ones on the right. It was surreal: I watched in dazed disbelief as a strange new world flitted before my eyes. The southern districts of the city thus crumbled, buildings tossed about like toys in the fierce winds created by the blast.

At the bottom of the stairs, staff mingled in front of the Savings Bureau, looking for all the world like ghostly apparitions as they stood in stunned silence, unable to comprehend what had happened. Several let out a cry when they caught sight of me; blood was streaming down my arm and rapidly forming a pool at my feet. Ms. Tomoyanagi immediately rushed to my aid. Wrapping her arms around my shoulders, she led me off to the Red Cross Hospital visible in the distance. The area between the Savings Division and the hospital had been cleared of buildings to create a firebreak.[5] There was nothing combustible in the area yet thick columns of flame, as if from large chimneys, rose here and there from the bare land. The earth was breathing fire!

"Fire, put out the fires!" shouted a man as he ran about frantically. "Water…" I began, but was ignored by Ms. Tomoyanagi who marched me onwards to the hospital.

No words can describe the sight that met our eyes at the Red Cross Hospital. It was like a scene from hell: people everywhere trying to push their intestines back into their ruptured abdomens, or, lacking the strength to do that, letting them trail as they walked; people covered in soot, the skin on their limbs shriveled and tattered or completely scorched black; people struggling to push their eyeballs back into their eye-sockets; people with faces and arms burned black and raw, their facial features indiscernible beneath massively swollen welts…everywhere people so badly burned all over their bodies that it was impossible to tell their age or gender, staggering about in silence, charred skin flapping down from their outstretched arms.[6]

Wherever I looked I saw people with just a small round of cropped hair on the crown of their heads. *Had they all just returned from the barbers? Even so, it's an odd-looking haircut,* I thought, until it finally dawned on me that the patch of hair on their heads was where their hats had been, the rest of their heads were burned down to the raw like their necks, faces, and bodies. *Surely these can't be real people…?* I thought. *How did they end up like this? What on earth happened? No, it can't be for real,* I concluded, *I must be dreaming!* Meanwhile, my

---

[5] As the war intensified, private houses and other buildings were demolished to create firebreaks to protect military facilities in the event of an air attack.

[6] Said to be a typical posture for people with severe burns as raising the arms prevents the burnt skin from rubbing painfully against other parts of the body.

nightmare was being flooded with more and more unearthly beings.

Ms. Tomoyanagi took me to the hospital waiting room and laid me down in the middle of the room. I was gradually losing consciousness; my eyelids began to droop and it was a struggle to keep them open. Ms. Tomoyanagi must have called a doctor. "She's in a bad way and losing a lot of blood. If you let her sleep, she'll die," I heard him say. As the sound of his footsteps faded, Ms. Tomoyanagi began loudly calling my name. A sweet drowsiness overcame me, dragging me down into a deep, dark ravine. Somewhere far above, Ms. Tomoyanagi's voice would drag me back up then gradually begin to recede again. And just when I thought she had gone for good, the sound of her voice would return, ever so distant at first then gradually drawing nearer and nearer. Sleep gripped me in its enticing embrace. Many times I thought, *Oh, please just let me be.*

How long did this go on for? Every time I was brought back to consciousness, I sensed more and more injured people around me; the air grew heavy and stuffy.

I was awoken with a jolt by a commotion. "The enemy planes have returned," people shouted. Ms. Tomoyanagi hoisted me up and began to drag me down to the basement for refuge. I could feel my legs, which were trailing behind me, bump down each and every step. I was laid down on the basement floor, on top of what felt like wooden slats. Though my mind was in a fog, I became aware that Ms. Tomoyanagi had a couple of female colleagues with her. Their voices drifted in and out. They appeared to be discussing what had happened, "Did a bomb hit the Savings Bureau?" "But how could that be, after the air raid warning was cancelled?"

I tried opening my eyes but even this proved too much for me and I slipped out of consciousness again. For some time, I drifted in and out of sleep. Eventually, in some deep recess of my body, a tiny spark of energy must have been revived. I was able to say a few words. "What on earth happened?" I murmured. My feeble query seemed to satisfy Ms. Tomoyanagi that I'd pulled through and she shed tears of relief. I tried to say more but she stopped me. "Hush now, it's okay, you're going to be alright," she said in soothing, motherly tones. Now that I was out of danger, her concern appeared to have shifted to her own mother.

"I'm going home to check on my mother. Once I've confirmed she's safe, I'll be right back so don't move, okay?" After repeating the promise to return, and begging her colleagues to look after me, she departed.

I wanted to speak with her, to say something, but my whispered query had left me so drained of energy I couldn't even muster up a 'thank you'. As I listened to her departing footsteps, I was filled with gratitude as well as an unbearable sense of loneliness. Once she had gone, I made no further attempts to open my eyes or speak. I could hear the voices of her companions, rising and falling endlessly like ripples on the water. I must have drifted off to their soft murmur.

"The hospital's on fire!" "Everyone out, quick!" I woke to a commotion and the strong stench of smoke.

"What'll we do about this girl?"

"We can't take her with us."

"But Ms. Tomoyanagi begged us to look after her."

"But we don't even know if we can get out ourselves with these dreadful injuries."

"What'll we do?"

The young women appeared to be at a loss over me. I vaguely sensed that I had narrowly escaped death. I could just manage to speak but had no energy to move. "Please go," I said, "I can't move."

"But..."

"It's okay, truly. Please leave me here and go." The two women hesitated for some time.

"We're sorry, so sorry. If only we were fit and well...but we can't carry you, injured as we are. Forgive us." After apologizing profusely, they finally departed. I wonder if the pair survived.

The basement seemed to be empty. I lay there in the empty silence amidst the faint smell of smoke and burning. Suddenly, a sharp smell hit my nostrils. It seemed that the fire had finally come round to me. I managed to force my eyes open a little. I could see light shining at the far end of the room, on the left. *Ah, so that's the exit,* I thought. As I watched, a new wave of smoke blew in as if on a gust of wind. At first the smoke was white and wispy but gradually it grew thicker and darker until finally it was billowing into the room like gigantic storm clouds. *When those clouds reach me, that'll be it*, I thought as I lay there awaiting impending death. I felt no suffering, no pain, nor fear. With death so close, I simply accepted my fate.

The black billowing clouds were almost upon me when a shadowy figure suddenly emerged from the smoke yelling, "Anyone else here? If there is, get out now!" The sound of his fierce, powerful voice propelled me to my feet. With no sense of the floor beneath me, I felt like I was walking on cloud as I made my way dazedly toward the door. As I did so, another figure emerged unsteadily from the smoke and came floating eerily toward me.

A gruesome face came into view: long, disheveled hair framing a deathly pale face that was smeared down one side with fresh blood, this too matted with hair. Out from beneath all the blood and matt, stared quivering, vacant eyes. I came to an abrupt halt, instinctively covering my face as I awaited the inevitable attack. Nothing happened. I spread my fingers and peeked furtively at the apparition. Was it not likewise peeking at me, a frightened look on its face? I drew closer and reached out; my hand hit the wall. A mirror; I had come face to face with myself!

I have a vague recollection of crawling through the smoke and climbing up the stairs to the ground floor. At the hospital entrance, I ran into a neighbor. He was standing on the stone steps at the entrance and staring outside as he pulled off tufts of a white cottony substance and stuck them on his body. *Odd behavior,* I thought but, delighted at finding someone I knew, I instinctively called out to him. "Hello, it's me, Fumiko. Kaneyuki, Fumiko."[7] He shot me a look then returned almost immediately to tearing up the cotton and slapping it on his limbs. "What are you doing?" He threw me another quick glance then sidled off without a word. After the war, we continued to live in the same neighborhood but neither of us ever spoke of our encounter that day. I later heard from my

---

[7] Kaneyuki is Bun's maiden name, Fumiko her real first name. Her penname 'Bun' is the name that she tends to be known by among her wide circle of friends at home and abroad.

mother that he passed away after succumbing to pneumonia at the age of eighty-one.

He was apparently one of her classmates at primary school and an old friend.

After the neighbor departed, I went out into the front garden. There were a handful of people sitting on the ground, forming a line as if waiting for treatment. I sat down behind them and gazed blankly over the city. *What on earth has happened?* I thought once again. Gone was the city that had been there in the morning; now there was nothing but flat land as far as the eye could see. I blinked several times, checking my eyes; they weren't mistaken, the city was obliterated. *Is this for real or a continuing nightmare?* I turned away and began to survey the scene around me. Charred bodies were strewn everywhere. People, burned black and raw, their heads and bodies so swollen it was impossible to distinguish their fronts from their backs, or determine their gender or age, were wandering around like ghostly apparitions, or lying on the ground, their bodies in tatters. Truly, everyone was like a dumbstruck, solitary lump of tattered rags. *No, they're not humans. It has to be a bad dream*, I thought.

I returned my gaze to the city. *What was my mother doing? Is it evening?* Everything appeared grey. *Mother is somewhere far off in the distance*, I thought, *on the other side of this colorless world.*

"Do you know how they've fared in Hakushima?" I asked the man sitting in front of me who was likewise surveying the city. He simply continued to stare blankly at the city and made no sign of replying.

"Which district of Hakushima do you refer to?" responded a young man behind me. "I have relatives in Hakushima. Their name is Murai."

"The Murais? The Murai family live in our neighborhood." We continued to chat for a while, about what I don't recall, when suddenly out of the blue he asked, "How old are you?"

"Fourteen." At my reply, he fell silent and, staring out at the crumbled city in the distance, made no further attempt to talk.

None of those lined up received any medical treatment, nor did it seem that anyone expected to. We all simply sat there staring vacantly at where there ought to have been a city. Eventually, the fires circled back round from behind the Red Cross Hospital. All those who could walk or crawl, fled. The city that had toppled, crumbled, and then disappeared was now ablaze. With no energy to walk or even crawl, nor the will to flee, I sought cover in the bushes in the front garden with the aid of the young man. He had a head injury and must have also been wounded in the chest as blood was seeping through a strip of cloth that had been wrapped haphazardly around his naked torso. He was able to walk but for some reason had no desire, it seemed, to escape.

Night fell. In the thick smoky darkness, people were being carried off on stretchers. It seemed they were all soldiers – the hospital must have been commandeered by the army at the time. "Sergeant Doctor, please help!"

"Can you stand up?"

"Yes."

The soldier appeared to have made it to his feet. "Good, then head in the opposite direction to the fires. And don't stop or that'll be the end of you!"

"No, Sir!"

"Sergeant Doctor!" another voice sounded in the dark. "Remove your hands from your stomach."

"I can't, or my guts will fall out!" It seems that they left this soldier behind. People groaned in pain as they lay there in the dark but no one, other than the soldiers, sought help. I wonder what happened to all those who fled or were taken away on stretchers. *Did they survive?*

The city continued to burn throughout the night. The fires swept over the Red Cross Hospital from behind. Thick flames roared from the windows of the concrete building. The fires whipped up a wind, which in turn whipped up the flames; the skies roared like thunder or the rumbling of the earth, while above our heads flames raged like the golden fires of hell. It was like a scene from another world. Huddled together under the bushes, the young man and I watched the horrific sight in stunned silence. Golden sparks rained down on us from the golden skies. Pine needles crackled in my ears, and I could hear my hair sizzling. The young man had found a sheet to protect us from the sparks. Huddled under the sheet, we watched the inferno in silence, totally mesmerized. I did not think about living or dying. That was something that the heavens would decide...

After some time had elapsed, the young man told me that his name was Iida Yoshiaki and that he was sixteen years old. "What are your hobbies?" he asked after learning my name.

"Reading," I replied at which he said that he too liked reading, reading and music.

"Music is the language of the gods," he said, and began to quietly tell me his story. That morning, he'd been at home with his younger sister when the bomb was dropped. He somehow managed to crawl out from under the collapsed house, but couldn't find his sister. He could faintly make out her cries coming from somewhere deep beneath the rubble and fought to push aside the slabs of broken roof and walls in order to get to her, but the neighbor's roof had collapsed onto their own and beneath that lay the walls. Old style lath walls were made from slender bamboo slats tied in a grid and then plastered with layer upon layer of clay. He would never have been able to break those with his bare hands. A further complication was that he couldn't actually see his sister, only hear her voice. As he desperately tried to dig her out from the rubble, flames began to appear around him.

"Argh, it's hot!" she screamed from beneath the crumbled house, "Pour water over me!" He ran to an emergency water tank nearby, filled a bucket and threw the water over the general area from which his sister's voice came. From his invisible sister came a feeble "Thank you." By now the flames were at his feet. His sister's screams rose, in gasps, from beneath the flames,

"Now go... please! Hurry!" The young man trailed off, unable to continue his story. Then, after some time, he murmured, "My sister was fourteen."

While escaping the fires, he managed to pull out a neighbor calling for help from a nearby house that had likewise collapsed. The woman's legs were injured. Hoisting her onto his back, he took her down to the shores of the river, where he found the area crowded with people fleeing the fires. Leaving her there, he waded across the river which must have been at low tide. He told me that his home was in Kawara, a district in

24

the southwest of the city but that his mother had been mobilized along with other housewives and was working at a factory in Ujina in the military port situated at the southernmost end of the city. En route to his mother's workplace, he must have also waded across Motoyasu River. When he reached the Red Cross Hospital, he found it crowded with people and decided to come in to see what was going on. It may well be that he had run out of energy, badly injured as he was in the head and chest.

He related his story in a quiet, calm tone of voice. In the light of the fires, I could see that his face wore a serene expression; it was a look of someone who had experienced extreme suffering. *Did I speak to him of anything?* As I listened to his soft tones, I grew drowsy and drifted into a peaceful sleep like a newborn baby.

I was woken by the cold. The fires raging above our heads had gone and with them, the golden light. We had been thrown into darkness, in the depths of which lay people's corpses. The groans of the dying bubbled up from among the dead and crept over the earth…

I realized that the sheet we'd been sharing had been folded in two and laid over my body; the young man had gone. A shiver of fear ran through me. It was the first time I'd felt afraid that day. Where had he gone? He was the only person I had to rely on now. With him gone, a growing sense of fear threatened to engulf me. Lacking the strength to stand, I tried scanning the area with my eyes from where I was sitting but he was nowhere to be seen. *Call him,* I told myself. *But what to call him?* I rolled the familiar term for a young male around quietly in my mouth before letting it out loudly, "*Oniisan!*" A live voice rang out over the dead and dying, then trailed off eerily into the distance. Its rawness so terrifying, I made no further attempts.

Inside the hospital waiting room the fires were still burning. Against the bright red flame-light, I could make out a dark silhouette. It was the young man! What on earth was he doing? He would bend down, then get to his feet, take several steps then bend down again. Moving slowly, a kettle in hand, one by one he was giving water to the dying – sad, tender movements, never stopping for a moment. "Music is the language of the gods," he had said but right at that moment it seemed to me that he was a god. Right then, he was the only person standing and walking on this earth. Relieved at finding him, I drifted off to sleep once more.

When I next woke, it was dawn and very cold. The remains of the city were submerged in a bluish smoky haze much as if we were in the depths of the sea. In the purplish mist and faintly blue-grey smoke, all was quiet. Not a single living being moved. Dawn had sprung on the city of the dead. The young man was sleeping quietly beside me. His face was very pale and there was a thick black trail of coagulated blood running down from his forehead. *He's dead*, I thought, my heart turning cold with fear. I gently touched his forehead. It felt cold as ice. I placed my palm near his nose and mouth to see if I could detect any breathing. Nothing! In desperation, I laid my head on his bare chest, pressing my ear close. Ever so faintly, from deep within, came the sound of a heartbeat. *He's alive!* I thought and was filled with pleasure. Just at that moment he opened his eyes. A smile flitted over his lips, then he said,

"I'm not going to make it. If you happen to survive, please tell my mother that I died here. She's working in the army ammunitions factory in Ujina."

"Don't die, oh please don't die!" I cried at which he merely gave a small shake of his head, as if to say 'I'm done for' and drifted off again. There was no sign on his face of sadness, fatigue or pain as he slept. Nevertheless, deeply anxious, I kept close watch over him. I could hear the faint sound of his breathing as he quietly slept. It was a very peaceful sleep as if he was accepting of whatever was to come his way.

It was the morning of August 7th, 1945. Gradually, dawn was breaking. Through the swirling mist, one after another, human rags were returning to the hospital. I suddenly felt parched, extraordinarily so, as if I had been without water for some time, months even. *Was there any water around?* I rose hesitantly to my feet. I could stand! Gingerly, I stretched my right leg out and took a step, then did the same with my left. I could walk! I scrambled out of the bushes and unsteadily wove my way around the edge of the shrubbery. Halfway round, I discovered a tap and had started tottering toward it when a large man lurched forward and virtually throwing himself on top of it, began to drink with loud, animal-like gulps. I noticed that his skull was split open; visible through the large crescent-shaped slit, was a light pulsing of russet-colored brain matter. *Goodness, he's alive!* I thought. Astonished, and moved, I waited for him to finish drinking.

Close behind me I could hear a man calling out someone's name as he searched among the hundreds of bodies covering the ground. Calling people by their names was probably the only way to find them as everyone was so badly burned it was impossible to make out their age, gender or any other such distinguishing features. I lacked the energy to turn my head and look over my shoulder at the man. As his voice gradually receded into the distance, I thought of my own father and whether he might also come looking for me. The man may well have been my father for, as I learned later, Father had indeed come to the Red Cross Hospital in search of me that day. Early on the morning of the seventh, while the city was still shrouded in darkness, he had woven his way through the smoke to the Savings Bureau. There he met a man who told him that all the female students had been taken to Ninoshima. That was all the information my father could obtain from the man. Ninoshima – often called 'Seto Fuji' on account of its beautiful conical shape – is a small island in the Seto Inland Sea, to the far west of the Savings Bureau.

Father was extremely downhearted and losing all hope of finding me alive after seeing the devastation on his travels through the city. And now he'd have to get a boat to cross over to Ninoshima. Having left family – my mother, badly injured brother, and grandparents – at Hakushima, he decided to put off going to the island until the following day. Instead he headed into the Red Cross Hospital grounds as it crossed his mind that I might just happen to be there. Just as he came to the tap near the bushes in the front garden, he apparently noticed a large man with his skull so badly split that the brain matter inside was clearly visible. *Ah, the poor man*, he'd apparently thought. *He probably only has two, three days at the most.* In the hospital grounds, he found people lying everywhere, naked and badly burned, their faces indistinguishable. And so he had begun calling me by name.

Another man, likewise searching for family, followed suit. Had it been my father's voice, or the voice of the other man that I'd heard? Barely alive, I was too dazed and feeble to tell at the time but when I think that my father saw the same large man in the same place and around the same time as me, it seems likely that the voice was my father's. Which means he must have passed right by without recognizing his own daughter – how different I must have looked! And I had lacked the energy to turn to look at him.

*Did I get to drink some water?* I think not. Seized suddenly by abdominal cramps, I had gone in search of some privacy. I couldn't find any shelter but found a quiet spot away from the main area to relieve my bowels; I had a terrible attack of diarrhea, my very first symptom of radiation-exposure.

Some way off, I saw a large crowd gathering around a cart that had appeared. I dragged myself over and found that they were giving out *kanpan*, the lightly baked wafer-like bread that the army used for emergency provisions. Father would tell me later that this cart wheeled up just as he arrived at the hospital. I was not the slightest bit hungry but took three packets, one each for me, my younger brother, and the young man Iida. My brother was a first-grader at primary school and like everyone else at the time, was always hungry. All we had for breakfast in those days was porridge made from the lees of soybeans, or what's left after the oil has been squeezed from the beans. No amount of servings of this could ever fill the stomach. There was no fish or meat, nor did we ever get to eat cakes, sugar, or anything that was sweet. My brother would be so happy to get some *kanpan*. I could almost see his thin, sunbaked face with its big bright eyes light up. But even those three little packets must have been too much for me to carry; by the time I returned to Iida, my hands were empty.

Iida must have been searching for me. He looked relieved as he walked up to me. I was greatly relieved too to see him up and about again. "Ujina, where my mother works, may have escaped the fires. Let's go there and get some treatment for your wounds. When you're feeling a little stronger, I'll take you to Hakushima." For the last day, he'd been my only source of support. I obediently followed him as he left the hospital. My blood-soaked trousers had dried as hard as a board and rubbed against my legs, chafing the skin as I walked. I vaguely recalled removing my blouse at some stage during the course of the previous day. Drenched and reeking of blood, it had become unbearably heavy. But as a young woman, I could hardly throw off my trousers. I hitched them up and held them away from my skin as I inched forward, one step at a time.

In front of the Red Cross Hospital had stood Hiroshima University of Liberal Arts and Science. We had watched it burn to the ground the previous night. Iida now made his way into the university grounds, trudging over the rubble before finally coming to a halt. For some time, he stood on the same spot, head bent, deep in contemplation. Lacking the strength to follow, I watched him from the street. He looked very lonely and sad as he stood there brooding.

Iida carried a water bottle slung around his neck. Perhaps I had complained of thirst for every time he saw water gushing from a broken water pipe, he would clamber over the rubble to put fresh water in the bottle. But I don't recall either of us drinking a single drop. In front of Hiroshima Tram Station, we found a horse lying dead on the tracks. It must have been only young for it had a beautiful glossy coat. Strangely, there were no signs of injury. *How could it have died?* From the previous day, I had seen countless corpses of people who had died from horrendous burns. The sight of the horse's strangely beautiful corpse made me stop in my tracks. A shiver ran through me. Iida gently urged me on.

A small cluster of houses behind the station and near Miyuki Bridge had survived the fires. My mother's paternal aunt lived in this vicinity. I asked Iida to wait near the bridge while I went to check on her. The roof of the house had collapsed but I found her alive in a small clearing among the rubble. She had a white bandage wrapped around her head, its whiteness almost painful to my eyes which for the last two days had seen nothing but burned, black objects. When she saw me, she sank to the floor and trembling all over, shuffled backwards recoiling from me. "I thought you were a ghost," she said when she finally realized who I was. She told me that my father had visited a mere thirty minutes before I arrived. "I simply can't find Fumiko," he'd said. "I'll have to give up the search for today and head back home." He had told her that everyone, including the Doi's, my mother's side of the family, was alive, though injured. I was the only one they hadn't managed to locate. *So they're all alive! My mother's alive!* I thought and was overcome with longing to see her.

Iida was waiting for me at Miyuki Bridge. I explained the situation, telling him that I would head back to Hakushima. He strongly protested. "You won't make it in your condition. Let's go to my mother's first and get some treatment for your injuries. As soon as you're a little stronger, I'll take you to Hakushima, I promise." Certainly, Ujina, where his mother was, was much closer than Hakushima on the far side of the city's burned plains. To get to Hakushima I would have to travel northwards across the still smoldering city to the opposite side of the city. But I was desperate to see my mother. Iida tried hard to convince me that I wouldn't make it but I kept insisting until he finally conceded.

"Take this," he said, pulling a jackknife from his pocket and holding it out to me. My eyes darted from his hand with the jackknife to his face, then back again. It suddenly dawned on me that he was a young man. Young women weren't supposed to associate with young men. Simply speaking to a member of the opposite sex, even if we were only students, would be seen as delinquent. But to accept gifts – now that would be scandalous! I rejected the knife with a shake of the head. He held it out to me once more. With another shake of my head, I turned and ran off. Or at least, in my heart I was running, in reality it was no doubt nothing more than a totter. He anxiously called after me but I staggered on. When I looked back after walking a considerable distance, I found him still standing at the bridge, his hand stretched out as before.

I walked and walked. The burned plains of the city stretched out as far as the eye could see. Smoke still rose here and there from the black rubble. And through this devastated landscape, ran a long, narrow, white road. *Keep heading north, north to Hakushima,* I repeated, urging myself on as I plodded along the white track. I felt certain that if I stopped walking, I would collapse on the spot. Along the way, I came across a solitary lamppost, burned black – in those days they were all made of wood – still standing among the rubble. *How could a wooden lamppost burned to tinder still be standing?* I thought as I fearfully tried to run past it – although of course, I couldn't actually run.

A little further on I found a skeleton in one of the tanks of water at the side of the road used for putting out fires in an emergency. It appeared to be the skeleton of a young woman; she was leaning against the side of the tank, her legs braced, cradling the skeleton of a young child in her arms. They'd evidently both been instantly turned from live flesh and blood into skeletons. The mother's head was bent as if to shield her child – probably only a newborn – a sad, tender air seemed to hover about her skull. I was greatly moved by the sight. At the same time, I found it strange that the skeletons hadn't crumbled. A lamppost burned to tinder still standing, skeletons frozen in poses of the living! Once again, I felt that I had drifted from reality into a nightmarish world.

I stumbled on, stopping every time I came across a water tank to look inside. I found skeletons in every single tank; skeletons standing as they leaned against the inner wall of the tank; skeletons huddled in the corners. Then there were the charred bodies of people who had only just made it as far as the water tank, or those hanging over the rim, their upper torsos inside the tank strangely burned to the bone while their lower torsos hanging on the outside were only partially burned. Tattered clothing – *or was it skin?* – hung from their bodies. The tanks were all bone dry. As if in a trance, I would stop at each and every water tank, look in, then walk on. Any desire to pray had long since left me.

Around the vicinity of Shirakami Shrine, I stopped coming across bodies. For a long time, I was puzzled as to why there were no bodies in this area when it was so close to the hypocenter. Then a few years back I watched the animated movie on the atomic bomb, 'Pikadon'. In the movie, there is a scene where the bomb explodes and instantaneously people and other objects are turned to dust and evaporate into thin air. I now believe that this is what happened. Some say that the Akatsuki Corps came through collecting the bodies the day after the blast but it was just after dawn that day when I walked through Shirakami and I saw no sign of any army brigade.

I have no idea how long it took me to get to Hakushima, nor what time it was when I arrived. I had not encountered a single living, moving creature on my travels across the city; no humans, no cats or dogs, no birds, no butterflies. Needless to say, there were no trees or plants swaying in the wind, nor any sound of any kind. It was literally a city of death. Eventually, I made it to Fukuya Department Store, near Hatchōbori. Its outer walls had burned down, leaving only a shell. I peered apprehensively inside but could see nothing in the dark interior. Had I been fit and well, Hakushima would have been a mere twelve or so minutes' walk from there. *Almost there!* I told myself. In the distance, I could make out the Communications Bureau with its distinctive L-shaped curve. What a comforting sight! Just beyond that L-shaped building was my home. I'd made it home, at last!

I followed the curve of the Communications Bureau and turned the corner. Staggering toward me from the opposite direction, leaning on each other for support, was a huddle of three. My eyes were immediately drawn to the large white shoes swamping the feet of the person in the middle. *Pure white!* I thought, surprised that the color white still existed in the world. Real live, walking people! I stopped, transfixed. They were the first living, moving beings I'd seen since parting with Iida in the morning. Or was it just another dream? Just as doubts began flooding in, one of the three cried out, "Hey, is that you Fumiko!" Though injured and mere shadows of their usual selves, there they all were, my mother, sister and Aunt Tomiko.

# My Mother and Brother Hideo

Mother was doing needlework when the atomic bomb fell. There was a whoosh followed by a brilliant flash of light then complete darkness. The next thing she realized the house had collapsed on top of her.

*A bomb!* she thought, her concern turning immediately to locating my younger brother Hideo who had not long left home for school. She tried to head outside but with each step her foot hit thin air and dropped to the ground beneath the house. The floor had collapsed! She noticed that her left hand was hanging limply from just above the wrist. Scanning the room for a bandage of some sort, she spotted the can of mandarins that I'd brought home the day before. It had burst open among the rubble, its contents spilled. Next to the can lay a strip of cloth. She wound this tightly around her wrist to hold it in place, then scrambled out from under the ruins just as Aunt Hatsuyo, my mother's older sister, arrived with Hideo on her back.

My brother Hideo was seven years old, a first-grader at primary school. It was the summer holidays but being one of the compulsory school attendance days,[8] Hideo's friend Miyo had come to pick him up and they'd headed off to school together. They were apparently playing on the monkey-bars in the school grounds when the searing rays from the explosion swept over them from behind, burning them badly all over, especially on the backs of their bare arms and legs right down to the soles of their feet and the very tips of their toes. The skin on their legs had curled up like grilled squid and hung down in

---

[8] In Japan, schools are normally closed for six weeks during the summer holidays; however, there are two or three days when pupils are required to attend so that teachers can check their homework, health and general wellbeing.

flaps. Nothing was left of their hair except for a round patch where their caps had been. Despite their injuries they tried to hurry home. As they raced out of the school gates, they ran into Aunt Hatsuyo.

Hakushima Primary formed a natural boundary between East Hakushima and West Hakushima and lay directly between Aunt Hatsuyo's house, in the east, and my mother's and maternal grandmother's houses in the west. My aunt had been heading west toward my grandmother's house to check if she was safe and had just reached the main gates of the school when Hideo called out to her. She hoisted him on to her back and ran toward my mother's. "Argh, my back's burning!" Hideo cried out in pain. Putting him down, she discovered that his clothes were aflame. She beat his clothing to smother the flames, then hoisted him onto her back and set off once more but she hadn't gone far before he apparently stopped her again: "Aunty, you're going the wrong way, our house is in that direction!" With nothing but collapsed houses every which way, she had completely lost her sense of direction.

At my grandmother's house, her elder son's wife and their one-month-old baby were buried alive under the house. Grandmother had been in the yard hanging out the washing and must have been shielded from the blast as she managed to escape without any burns. But her daughter-in-law had been inside at the time, feeding the baby in the drawing room, and the house had collapsed on top of them. "Help, quickly, Matsuko and Masakatsu are pinned under the house!" she screamed frantically when my mother and Aunt Hatsuyo rushed round.

Just then, Aunt Tomiko, my mother's younger sister, arrived home from the bank where she worked. She had left home in the morning, catching the tram to work as always. The tram had travelled some two or three hundred meters down the track and was just nearing Shukkeien Park when the bomb exploded leaving her with serious wounds to the back of the head. The area around the park was flattened – some say this was because the blast whipped up a tornado. The train with my aunty on it was blown from its rails. For some time afterwards, the carriages lay on the road where they had fallen, a blackened wreck.

My half-sister, Mitsuko, was in the kitchen at my grandmother's when the bomb fell. She would later recount how, in the blinding flash of light, she saw every single tiny clod of dirt in the garden rise momentarily from the ground. The next moment she was hurled from the house into the next-door neighbor's kitchen. She suffered grievous facial injuries.

Everyone set about rescuing Aunt Matsuko and the baby from underneath the house. "They're under here," screamed my grandmother. They began digging where she pointed – in the absence of any sound from mother and child, this was all they had to go by.

Finally, they managed to break a hole in the clay wall and had just pulled the baby to safety when the fires came round. The baby's mouth and nostrils were filled with dirt which Grandmother washed free with some water from the emergency water tank. Meanwhile, they had succeeded in partially digging out Aunt Matsuko but were struggling to free her lower torso. "If you don't help us Matsuko, we'll be forced to flee without you!" they warned as the fires crept closer and closer. Eventually, she was rescued. The next day she quietly slipped down to the paddy fields at the evacuation center where they'd fled, to wash her underwear in a little rivulet – she'd apparently soiled them in all the exertion of trying to free herself. Aunt Matsuko subsequently survived until nearly 90 years of age, but she had a hard life, losing her husband, my uncle, in the blast and plagued with chronic back pain for the rest of her life.

The fires drove them all the way down to Chōjuen Park, near the river, where they found the banks teeming with people. Mother climbed the concrete steps leading up from the embankment and sat down near the top with my brother cradled in her arms. "Argh, my back's burning, burning hot," Hideo cried in much pain and pleaded unrelentingly for water. People sitting on the riverbank scooped up water in their hands and passed it along a line of hands until it finally reached my mother, little more than a dribble by then.

Thankful nevertheless, she pressed her damp palm to my brother's lips.

My brother's friend Miyo was likewise badly burned and her skin hung in tatters from her body. She had fled with my family to the river and waded across it with my mother, Aunt

Tomiko, and sister as they headed to what appeared to be a first aid tent erected on a site used by the Engineering Corps for military training.

The moment the doctor removed the bandage binding my mother's wrist she passed out to the sound of my sister's screams, "Mother, please don't die!" Next it was my sister's turn; the doctors peeled off the blood caked on her wounded and swollen face, only to set off the bleeding once more. Aunt Tomiko, with the severe head injuries, had mercurochrome antiseptic applied to her wounds but the doctors didn't remove the hundreds of shards of glass embedded in her scalp. She carefully ran her fingers over her head feeling for glass splinters with her fingertips and pulling them out along with bits of entangled flesh. A little antiseptic and dressing of the wounds, that was the full extent of the treatment they received.

On the way back, my aunt and others stopped, overcome with exhaustion, to rest under a tree. The surrounding riverbanks were strewn with human rags. Miyo was too weak to go any further. "Miyo-chan, you wait here. We'll look for your mother and tell her where you are," they promised as they rose to their feet, although it was uncertain whether they would be able to make it back to the park, or indeed, what was to become of them.

"I'll look after her for you," offered a man nearby. Reassured, they set off again but Miyo called out after my aunt, "*Oneechan, oneechan!*" The sound of her feeble cries tore at Aunt Tomiko's heart and the memory still brings tears to her eyes. They ran into several neighbors on the embankment, on Nakagawara and later at the evacuation site, but they never came across Miyo's mother.

Later, when we were living in a hut we had built on the burned-out remains of our home and struggling to survive, a young returned serviceman came to visit us. He was Miyo's father. My grandmother told him all she knew while he listened with bent head. "Thank you," he said when she finished. "Miyo is the only one in the family I've heard news of. I'll go down to the area where you left her under the tree and see if I can find out more." He left, shoulders hunched and downcast, then returned in the evening with a small box in his hands. "This contains Miyo's ashes, I scooped them up from among the ashes of the dead cremated there," he explained. The sight of him forlornly clutching the little box and his voice as he spoke these words remain etched in my memory.

Whenever my mother talked about the bombing and touched on Miyo, she would break down in tears. "Poor Miyo was covered in burns, just like Hideo, but your grandmother was carrying Masakatsu who was only seven months old at the time, and everyone else was too badly injured to carry her on their backs. And then there was nothing more I could do with a broken arm and Hideo on my back. She clung to my clothes and tried to follow us, poor dear, just imagine how her mother would have felt had she witnessed that." Mother blamed herself for not taking Miyo with them.

Down at the park by the river where they'd fled that day of August the sixth, my mother and family were hit by torrential rain and then, when some enemy planes flew over, everyone dived into the river for cover. It had been high tide but it must have turned for people were being swept away. There was an old woman whom people rescued from the water time and time again only to find that she'd gone back into the river. Eventually she was swallowed up and dragged away with the tide.

"Let's see," my mother would recount, "there were maybe a thousand or more people lying packed together on the riverbanks. A group of young women – goodness knows where they'd been working – were all stark naked, the skin hanging off their badly burned limbs. Soldiers were walking through, gently placing strips of cloth or paper over the women's loins." We found out later that the neighbor's daughter was among them. "They all passed away in the night or, in some cases, the following day...poor souls," she would say shedding tears whenever she recalled those events.

My brother was laid down with the others on the riverbank. "I'm scared! Please put something over me!" he cried, terrified of his nakedness. My father gathered grass to cover him but it soon fell off as he writhed in agony. Father would replace the grass, only to see it fall off time and again, and so the long night dragged on. Next morning, before sunrise, my father left in search of me.

What time was it? The hot mid-summer's sun was beating down on the sea of scorched people when a rumor began to spread that treatment could be found at the Communications Bureau Hospital, some twenty or so minutes' walk away. My grandfather, Aunt Tomiko, mother, and sister – the only members of my family at the river who could still walk – set off up the embankment. My mother was in bare feet, having been at home inside at the time of the blast. The ground on the embankment was so hot it seared the soles of her feet. Along the path up the embankment, they came across the large body of a dead man. Noticing the shoes on his feet, my grandfather chanted a sutra and said, as he put the man's white shoes on my mother's feet, "Please forgive me for taking your shoes for my daughter." He then sat down on the spot and refused to walk any further; he'd given up on the idea of going to the hospital. My aunt and sister had serious head and facial injuries, they linked arms on either side of my mother and all three set off together.

They were the three 'living, moving people' that I ran into just as I made it to the Communications Bureau next to the hospital, after traversing on foot the burned wasteland of Hiroshima City. The large, white shoes swamping my mother's feet caught my attention first; such a vivid white it stung my eyes, which, as related earlier, had seen nothing but blackened, bloody bodies and dark scorched earth from the time of the blast.

I joined my mother, aunt, and sister and headed to the hospital but we found things just as horrendous there as they had been at the Red Cross Hospital. Given the situation, there was little likelihood of our receiving any treatment. Later I heard that the Hospital Director, Doctor Hachiya, had been seen en route to the hospital from his home in Hakushima after the blast hit. People found him lying on the roadside in such a bad state that no one would have recognized him had it not been for his cries of "I'm Hachiya from the Communications Bureau Hospital, please take me there." Apparently, despite his injuries, he worked with the few surviving nurses at the hospital to treat the wounds of the injured. The day we visited, however, we waited for some time before eventually giving up and leaving the horrific scenes of suffering behind us. Doctor

Hachiya later wrote a book of his experiences – *Hiroshima Nikki* (Hiroshima Diary) – the very first such memoir to be written by a physician.

Unsuccessful in our attempt to receive medical treatment, we turned toward home. All around us was nothing but burned-out fields. It was impossible to make out where our house had been. Here and there crooked water pipes poked up from the ground. "This is Nishioka's well, which means that the water pipe here is for Nishioka's house, and the one over there is Kodama's..." We clambered over the rubble, coming to a standstill where we thought our own house had been; the entire area was scorched a deep reddish-black giving the appearance that it was still smoldering. There had been houses here, and until yesterday, people had been living in them. Now, all that could be seen was a wasteland. We stood there in stunned silence.

My grandmother and Aunt Hatsuyo's house had been only a few doors down from ours, overlooking the fenced surround of Hakushima Primary School. A few bricks of the school fence still stood among the rubble and on them, written in large letters in charcoal, were the words 'Fumiko, head to Saka'. My father must have written them as he left in the morning. I suspect that, had I read this message before meeting up with my mother, aunt, and sister, I would have collapsed on the spot from sheer exhaustion.

We staggered back in silence to the river where we were met by my uncle and grandmother who explained that everyone else had fled to Hesaka Primary School, the designated evacuation site for residents in Hakushima Ward. The school lay four kilometers to the north. "They've taken the badly injured, including Hideo, to the center by boat. We stayed back to let you know." Shortly after that, my uncle, who was gravely wounded, was loaded onto a boat and taken away with my grandmother in tow. This left just four of us to walk to the school; me, Aunt Tomiko, my sister whose facial wounds had affected her sight, and my mother with her limp, broken arm.

In the distance, we could see the rope bridge used by the Engineering Corps to traverse the river but, lacking the energy to go that far, we decided to wade across, the river fortunately at low tide. The cool, clear water was soothing to our hot bodies. Nevertheless, it was up to our thighs in the middle and we were in danger of being swept away as we staggered across. Eventually we made it to the other side and dragged ourselves up onto the bank. On the path lay a black, charred corpse. It was facing upwards, its head pointing toward the river. There were no eyes, nor teeth showing in the gaping mouth, just dark cavities where they ought to have been. There was a youthful air about the splayed arms and legs and I guessed it was the body of a nine or ten-year-old boy. But why would he have been here on his own at the time of the blast? He was unlikely to have fled or been carried here afterwards. The only explanation was that he'd been instantly incinerated in the heat of the blast. Even so, how was it that he'd fallen face up with his head lying in the direction of the epicenter? I stood for some time gazing in amazement at the boy's body.

We had four kilometers to walk. With the sun blazing down on us, the path along the embankment felt inordinately long – a red-dirt path stretching as far as the eyes could see with not a single tree to provide shade. "Hesaka Primary, Hesaka Primary," we chanted to ourselves as we dragged each foot forward, gasping in the withering heat. Just as the houses in Hesaka came into view, we came to a large tree. It threw a cool dark shade over us as we collapsed under it one by one. We lay there inert, except for mother who pressed on, anxious about my younger brother.

On her way, mother ran into a friend who said to her, "The Murai's son, Hiroshi, has just passed away but your young lad is still alive!" Hiroshi was fourteen. He had been working in the fields, under the student mobilization scheme, at the time of the blast. On hearing that Hideo was still alive, my mother rushed ahead to the school but by the time she reached the area where my brother was lying, deep inside the school grounds, he had already departed for the heavens.

"Madam, call out to him, he may still be able to hear you, he's only just departed," said a young sick and injured soldier nearby, trying to console her. She gathered my brother in her arms, shook him and called his name but he never opened his eyes. She was overcome with grief. When she eventually glanced around at the young soldier who had watched over my brother she found that he too had quietly departed this world.

My poor brother Hideo, his life robbed by the atomic blast after just seven short years in this world. From the time he was old enough to remember, the war had turned for the worse and people were constantly hungry. There was not enough of the staple food rice to go around, let alone anything sweet to eat. High school students and housewives had been mobilized to work in factories and the like, while primary school pupils from grade three upwards were evacuated to rural areas far from the city.

In my family, my younger sister and other younger brother, who were fourth and sixth-graders respectively, were evacuated with a large group of school children to a temple in the countryside, leaving only my younger brother Hideo, a first-grader, and myself, a high school student, at home. My parents left home early each morning, my father for work, my mother as a 'volunteer housewife', leaving me to lock up the house on my way out. I would stay at home with Hideo as long as possible but I wasn't able to wait until Hideo's school opened. Invariably, he would have to hang around outside school killing time with friends until classes started.

Down the road from our house, on the corner en route to Hakushima Primary, was a stationery store called Nishino. In front of the store sat a large round rock. After school, once he'd finished playing with his friends, Hideo would sit down on this rock and wait for my mother or me to return. How cold and lonely he must have felt waiting there on his own as the sun sank and the cool evening breeze ushered in dusk. Of all my memories of Hideo, this image of his solitary figure sitting on that rock is the most poignant.

Later I heard more about Hideo's friend Miyo and her family from Natchan – also seven years old at the time of the blast – who used to go to school with Hideo and Miyo. Miyo's family had lost their home in the massive firebombing of Tokyo[9] in March that year. After tossing up whether to go to

---

[9] On the night of March 9, 1945, the U.S. launched a massive air attack on Tokyo using thousands of incendiary bombs that caused utter devastation. The actual number of deaths and other casualties remain unknown but conservative estimates state around 100,000 were killed with at least an equal number wounded. Vast areas of

Chiba or Hiroshima, they eventually chose Hiroshima on account of Chiba's proximity to Tokyo. They stayed for some time with Natchan's family who had a large rented home with a good number of rooms and occasionally took in boarders. When a house came available nearby, after the family living there moved to Manchuria to be with their son, Miyo's family moved in. There were six children in her family, the three oldest were all male and had been evacuated under the government scheme. The remaining three were all girls, the youngest, a baby not yet walking. On the day of the blast, Hideo and Miyo had gone to collect Natchan but finding her in bed with an upset stomach, they continued on to school without her. Gazing at the sky from where she lay in bed, Natchan had said to her grandmother close by, "A B29 dropped a parachute!" The next thing she knew she'd been hurled from her bedroom into the next-door neighbor's house. Her younger sister was buried alive under the rubble. Together with her mother she managed to dig her sister out but at some stage lost sight of her mother. Hoisting her wounded sister onto her back, she fled with her grandmother who was complaining of pain, her ribs having been broken.

As they fled to the river, they heard Miyo's mother calling for help from under their collapsed house. They could also hear the baby crying but there was nothing they could do. The riverbanks were inundated with people when they arrived. A man called out to Natchan, "Please rip up my shirt and use it to get me some water." Natchan tore a strip off his shirt, dipped it in the river and wrung the water out into his open mouth.

"He'll die if you give him water," warned people nearby but she took no heed; he was already on the verge of death. Natchan carried her sister across the river, wading her way through swollen corpses that were being swept downriver by the current.

As recounted earlier, all those who had been working outside at the time of the blast were left with a small round of short hair – in those days, all the men had short shaven heads – where their caps had been while the rest of their heads were

---

Tokyo were destroyed, and more than one million residents are said to have fled the city.

badly burned. Like me, Natchan was puzzled by their strange haircuts and wondered if they had all gone to get haircuts at the same time. She also struggled to understand why they were all wearing long-sleeved shirts in the middle of summer; it was not shirt sleeves but burned skin flapping down their arms.

Natchan has since married and now lives in Chiba. She told me that she never goes home to Hiroshima on or around the sixth of August because, she explained, her mother said to her, "Don't you ever come back to Hiroshima on August the sixth. People look at you and are reminded of their own children whom they lost in the blast." This called to mind what she used to say whenever she met my mother:

"Mrs. Kaneyuki, you must be reminded of Hideo every time you see me, right? I'd like to visit you more often but...well, I find it painful too."

After the blast, our families were next-door neighbors and on very good terms. Natchan would always try to cheer up my mother who was often sickly. "Take care and stay well, Mrs. Kaneyuki. My mother would be lost without you!" she would say. I think our mothers were the same age. When her mother passed away she said to my mother, "Mrs. Kaneyuki, you need to live a long life to make up for my mother's lost years. From now on, I'll think of you as my mother." Natchan had a busy life as a housewife and hairdresser but still managed to grow a vegetable garden and send us her home-grown sweet potatoes, one of my mother's favorite foods.

"They've all died, haven't they," Natchan would often say. "They say five thousand survivors of the bomb die every year. Now there are only the younger ones, like you and me, left. I'm still working but when I do retire, I'd like to do something useful for the survivors, or to tell people about the bombing of Hiroshima." She is now 74 years old.

She has a busy life tending for her husband who suffers from dementia.

At the end of the war, my mother put her injured arm in a sling and, while battling various symptoms of radiation poisoning, supported her family. Obtaining food for the family was a daily struggle. Our possessions had been sent to the countryside for safekeeping. Little by little, much like peeling the skin from bamboo shoots, they were sold in exchange for food and it wasn't long before we ran out of things to sell. The daily reports at the time spoke of deaths in Hiroshima not only from the blast but also from starvation.

"Tomorrow it will be us!" my father would say as he stared at his bowl of gruel containing little more than clear hot water, "But don't let the hunger show on your faces when you die, okay? Go with a smile!"

My mother would leave home early in the morning, after a glass of water and nothing else, her objective being to go around the local farms, begging for food. She would return after dark, mentally and physically exhausted, and slump to the floor, an empty *furoshiki* in her lap. "Do you know, I got down on my hands and knees on the dirt path in the fields and bowed so low my forehead scraped the ground, begging them for just a few dud potatoes even. 'Please', I said, 'my children are starving.'"

Despite the difficulties, my family often laughed. "How is it that we can always hear laughter coming from your house?" people in the neighborhood would ask in wonder. Mother was the sunshine in our lives. And then children were free to do whatever they liked once they'd finished the daily task of gathering charcoal; Hiroshima's burned-out ruins provided fertile grounds for discovery and adventure games so there was never a shortage of things to talk about at home.

My father's sciatica gave him dreadful pain but he nevertheless cleared the rubble around our hut to plant strawberries and vegetables, and once he'd done that he tilled the land where the preschool had been, creating a proper vegetable garden. But we had no income and inflation had rendered all of our pre-war savings worthless.

Two years after the war, I got a job. I was sixteen. My meager salary provided a regular income for our family of five. My older sister, who had been raised by my grandmother, likewise worked to support her grandmother, aunt, and aunt's child after they lost Uncle Torao, the main provider for the family. My other brother, a junior high school student, found part-time work making bamboo strips for lath walls, a job that left his hands constantly cut and bleeding. The two men he went to work with were exuberant young men and they filled

44

our house with laughter when they dropped in most days for a chat.

Father's sciatica pain must have been considerable for it wasn't uncommon for us to be woken in the night by the sound of his groans. Even so, each day he would make his way to a garden plot at his mother's house in Saka, resting every five meters or ten minutes along the way, and little by little he raised some sweet potato for us. My mother set up a stand near the Communications Bureau selling the baked sweet potato, *yakiimo*. The customers, mostly employees at the Bureau, would crowd around my mother who was very popular with her warm, bright disposition, and the stand did very well.

My father and brother were the ones tasked with lugging the potatoes into the city from Saka every day. There were always police on the train on the lookout for peddlers and black marketeers. My brother was a bit of a rascal and caused my mother many headaches but he was also astute and often managed to get them safely past the police. There were times, however, when he was caught off guard and all their potatoes would be confiscated, to the bitter disappointment of my mother who would be waiting expectantly with a cart at the station for their return. The next day the stand would be closed and there would be no income.

And then at the time of *o-bon* and *o-higan*, during the spring and autumn equinoxes, my mother, brother, sister, and I would sell flowers in front of temples for people to take on their customary visit to the family grave. I would rush home after helping with the early morning sales, quickly change, and then head off to work. Meanwhile, I suffered from a strange affliction that was gradually worsening. My lips, both upper and lower, would become inflamed and fester making it difficult to eat, while the pain kept me awake at night. Eventually, I was hospitalized for treatment. The hospital was housed in a large wooden military building surrounded by grassy fields in a place called Hiro, roughly one hour's train-ride from Hiroshima.

The doctors struggled to identify my illness. They tried various treatments, including radium therapy; a stick of radium would be cut to roughly the same width as my mouth and taped to my lips. I used to go around the other rooms in the hospital, radium stick glued to my lips, visiting my sick friends. Some years later, this treatment hit the headlines in the newspapers; patients like myself were spreading radiation as they moved about, the papers said. The radium burned my lips a deep black.

Around that time, I received some hopeful news from Doctor Hachiya, the Director of Hiroshima Communications Bureau Hospital. "When I went to a conference in Tokyo, someone gave a paper on an illness exactly like yours Fumi-chan," he wrote. "I've asked them to treat you so please go immediately to Tokyo Communications Bureau Hospital." Heaven knows where mother got the money to buy a train ticket for me. In those days, it was a twenty-three-hour ride by steam train to Tokyo. I kept a mask over my mouth throughout the trip. Mother sat opposite me on the train. She was already suffering from heavy bleeding due to uterine fibroids or what may have been cancer. After six months in hospital I was well enough to go home. By the time I returned to Hiroshima, my mother was greatly weakened. She told me she had been bleeding heavily the entire time I was away. "I just kept telling myself, you've got to hang in there, at least until Fumi-chan gets back!" she said.

Mother was operated on. My siblings and I provided the blood for a transfusion as my father suffered from chronic anemia. We took a portable cooker and pots into the hospital so that we could feed and look after her. After she was sent home to rehabilitate, mother stopped taking the medication explaining that she would only have to go and buy more when it ran out and that we didn't have the money for that. It was true, with only my income there wasn't enough money to go around. Hidden inside the pages of my brother and sister's high school textbooks were numerous invoices from the school requesting payment of school fees. They never breathed a word of this and eventually my younger sister decided to quit school and get a job. "Mikio's a boy so he's got to at least finish high school," she explained.

Despite these illnesses and years of extreme poverty, my mother managed to live a very long life of over ninety years. On August 2nd when she was ninety-two, she was suddenly struck down by a stroke and rushed by ambulance to hospital. It was only a light stroke and she was soon moving her limbs and talking again but two days later, she drifted away, as if in a sleep, without the nurse even noticing. The previous day, when the nurse appeared, my mother had sat up in bed and bowing her head low, thanked her for having looked after her. The nurse looked across at me and said with a smile, "Your mother's gone dotty again."

That same day I had sat all day with mother, holding her hand. When evening came around and I stood up to go home, she said, "It's lonely on my own." So I returned to my seat at the side of the bed and clasped her hand. We must have sat in silence like that for about an hour before I said, rising to my feet, "I'll come again tomorrow."

"I want to say goodbye," my mother said, struggling out of bed. Thinking that she just wanted to see me to the elevator now that she had regained movement, I shrugged off her talk about 'saying goodbye' – much like the nurse had smiled at her talk earlier. But that really was her final goodbye to me.

# Father's Story

One can never predict one's fate! On the morning of August 6th, father boarded a bus at Hiroshima Station in order to go to Saka, a town in Setouchi where his mother lived. He normally hated taking the bus but that particular morning he boarded one that was departing five minutes earlier than the train. Hiroshima Station was especially badly hit by the blast and had father been waiting for the train as usual, he would have been there at the time and almost certainly perished, leaving no trace.

The bomb exploded not long after the bus departed, just after it crossed the railway line at Ōzu, on the eastern side of the city. Fortunately, no one was hurt; it seems the bus was shielded as it passed in the shadow of a large building. "Please take us to Kure!" cried the passengers so the driver planted his foot on the accelerator and, leaving the city behind, raced eastwards along the highway at breakneck speed. Kure was a military port some twenty-six kilometers east of Hiroshima.

Anxious about family, father wanted to turn back but no amount of imploring would convince the driver to stop to let him off. He had resigned himself to being taken to Kure when, just as they approached Saka, they were brought to a halt by a large brine cart abandoned in the middle of the road, its carriers having fled. When the driver disembarked in order to remove the cart from their path, father seized the opportunity to jump off with him. Looking back across the sea in the direction of Hiroshima, he saw an enormous mushroom-shaped cloud billowing in the sky, a raging ball of fire at its vortex.

*That's no ordinary bomb*, he thought, uneasily. In the past, he had been to China as an army civilian, but never had he seen or heard of such a strange blast.

Father went firstly to his mother's house. Her storm doors had been blown off in the blast but she was safe and well, and delighted by his unexpected visit. "As you see I'm fine but I'm going to head back to Hiroshima to look for everyone." So saying, he set off at a jog in the direction of Hiroshima.

In those days a large military training ground, called the East Parade Ground, stretched northwards from the current Shinkansen or north entrance to Hiroshima Station, and the square in front of it, all the way to Mt. Futaba. When father reached the military complex he found the grounds strewn with injured people, so many there was barely room to walk. He froze in horror, unable, for a time, to go any further. The bodies on the ground were so badly mutilated they no longer appeared human; indeed, it was impossible to tell whether they were dead or alive.

Father felt almost certain we would be lying among the injured, so often had he reminded us to flee in the case of an emergency to Nigitsu Shrine – a large shrine nestled in the hills on the western side of Mt. Futaba, adjacent to the military training grounds. In search of family, he walked among the bodies on the training grounds, carefully checking the faces, appearance and build of each and every one. Living or dead, all were burned beyond recognition, leaving no trace of age, gender, or facial features. Many were denuded, but it would have been impossible, in any case, to identify family among those who had retained some vestiges of clothing, so bloody and coated in ash were they. Father would recount later how he went to the extraordinary lengths of prying in the mouths of the dead to check the alignment of their teeth. And so he went, back and forth, east to west, west to east, scrutinizing the faces of each and every person lying on the ground. How he regretted telling everyone to flee to the Shrine in an emergency!

The sun was coursing down the sky toward the west when he spotted Uncle Torao, my mother's brother, staggering in the crowd. "*Niisan!*" he called. "Ah, Masao…I want to go home but where am I? And what on earth has happened?" Father said that uncle seemed greatly befuddled, like someone with dementia. We discovered later that he had been only three-hundred or so meters from the hypocenter when the bomb exploded, and while he had miraculously survived the blast, it had left him with a massive brain hemorrhage. He died in agony, his head hammering, seventeen days later on the twenty-third of August. He had apparently complained of a headache and was unsteady on his feet when father met him the day of the blast. Father found a stick for him to use as a prop and led him away from the crowds to a clearing on the western boundary of the parade grounds. Leaving him there briefly, he returned with a straw mat that he'd found and said, as he handed it to my uncle,

"I'm going to search for family again. Please stay here. If I'm not back by nightfall, please use this mat as bedding and get some sleep."

After that, father continued to search the grounds for family members but to no avail. Deciding to head home, he returned to the spot where he'd left my uncle only to find him gone; no doubt he'd given up waiting for father and gone off in search of family himself. Father said that when he relocated him, he no longer carried the straw mat or walking stick. He took uncle with him as he headed toward Hakushima. They came to Nigitsu Shrine, where father left uncle waiting again on the side of the road at the entrance while he went into the shrine precincts to look for family. On either side of the path leading up to the shrine was a line of large stone lanterns. All had crumbled. At the sight of them, father said that he lost all hope for us.

Past Nigitsu Shrine and under the Sanyō Line railway bridge was Tokiwa Bridge and, beyond that, Hakushima where we lived. And just several doors down from our house was Uncle Torao's house, my mother's family home. Near the east end of Tokiwa Bridge stood a large restaurant called Taikarō. As father and uncle approached the bridge, they saw the Taikarō engulfed in a raging inferno, sparks raining down all around. Father considered finding another straw mat, soaking it in the river and using it as cover to get past the fire but it wasn't feasible with my uncle in tow.

Instead, they headed down to the banks of the river, which were packed with evacuees. Father spotted a small boat moored to the bank. Leaving uncle on the bank, he leaped in, intending to use it to cross the river. Others on shore quickly followed suit and in no time the boat was crammed with people. "Please, we'll sink unless some of you get off." No one budged. Relenting, he said, "I've never rowed a boat before but I'm prepared to give it a go. But please, no one must move an inch!" The rim of the boat was barely above the water line. Everyone sat stock still, hardly daring to breathe – how desperate they must have felt!

They somehow managed to reach the other side where they found the shore similarly crowded. That was where father ran into his father-in-law, my maternal grandfather. Grandfather was a born optimist; despite the catastrophic situation, father found him chuckling and chatting loudly, as always, with the people around him. Later that evening, father was also reunited with my mother, younger brother and my grandmother's household on an island upstream commonly known as Nakagawara. The embankment area on the Hakushima side, where the Ōta River splits into two, is called Chōjuen Park and is famous for its flowering cherries. Mid-stream was a large island; this is what was called Nakagawara.

Nakagawara was owned by the Engineering Corps. Civilians were not permitted on the island, though a narrow wooden bridge connected it to the embankment. Fearful though we were of being caught by soldiers, we rarely saw anyone using the island and so we often took the bridge over to its fields of tall grasses and wild flowers, which were an ideal playground for children. Mother told us of how when she was a little girl, all the relatives used to gather in the fields for picnics, armed with a feast of homemade food just like at cherry-blossom viewing parties. The island had thus seen more elegant times, but for us as children it was simply an army base and on the day of the atomic bomb blast, it became the final resting place for the masses of people who, close to death, laid themselves down, covering the ground in bodies.

As an aside, today only a tiny strip of the island is visible above the muddy waters. Several trees have taken root there and tower high into the sky, providing a sanctuary for flocks of wild birds.

Alongside the island was a rope bridge that stretched from Chōjuen Park in Hakushima to the opposite banks of Ushita town. Called the Engineering Corps Bridge, because it likewise belonged to the Engineering Corps, it was out of bounds to civilians. Beneath the bridge on the Hakushima side of the river, the riverbed must have been dug out especially deeply for the current slowed there forming a vast, fathomless pool of beautiful emerald green waters. I was often tempted to cross that stretch of water, swinging the long bridge as I went. One day, making up my mind to do so, I crawled under the rope closing it off to pedestrians, mounted the bridge and stood there gazing down at the pool of water. How mysterious it looked from directly overhead! A strange and frightening sensation came over me as if my entire being was melting, phantom-like, into the emerald green waters, and being sucked into the pool's watery depths.

On the day of the blast, I saw a young boy's charred body at the opposite end – the Ushita end – of the bridge.

"Whatever you do, don't evacuate to Chōjuen Park, the Engineering Corps keep their horses there," my father used to warn but that's precisely where Mother and other members of my family fled, driven by the fires, to Chōjuen Park and Nakagawara. When evening came round, grandmother spotted a man crossing the rope bridge. "Hey, it's Masao! Masaaaoo!" she cried, calling out to my father. Our neighbors had also fled to Nakagawara. Mr. Takahashi who lived directly behind the Doi's, my mother's family, helped bring my uncle and grandfather there. And so it was that my entire family was reunited – everyone, that is, except me.

That evening was cold. Everyone covered themselves with long grass they gathered for warmth. My seven-year-old brother Hideo, who had been critically injured in the school grounds, his back burned by the searing heat of the blast, was frightened by his nakedness. "I'm scared...please put something over me," he cried. Father gathered grass to cover his burned body but it kept slipping off as he writhed about in pain. Each time it fell off, my father would gather the grass up again and cover him, and so this continued throughout the night.

The next day, August 7th, father left before dawn in search of me, travelling across the burned plains from Nakagawara in the northern part of the city, to the Savings Bureau in the southern districts. Mother, my sister, Aunt Tomiko, and grandfather also left Nakagawara saying they would head to the Communications Bureau Hospital. When my badly injured brother was loaded onto a boat and evacuated to Hesaka

Primary School, Uncle Torao, nursing serious injuries, and grandmother, who was looking after him, stayed behind to let us know. Before the day was over, Hideo rose, all alone, to the heavens.

On the morning of the eighth of August, father roped Hideo's dead body to him and set off over the hills for Saka, where his mother, my paternal grandmother, lived. He hadn't long departed when he was back again; rigor mortis had set in, impeding his movements. He borrowed a cart from a local farmer and laid my brother in it. Lying face-up in the small wooden cart, Hideo looked for all the world like a sleeping angel – his face was completely unscathed although he had been badly burned from head to foot on the back of his body.

After we saw Hideo off in the wooden cart, we headed off on foot in the direction of Hiroshima Station on the off chance that the trains would be running. There were nine of us in all, Aunt Tomiko, my mother, sister, and me – we had been reunited the previous day after I made my way back to Hakushima – my maternal grandparents, Uncle Torao, Uncle Torao's wife and their seven-month-old baby. It was evening by the time we reached the inner city. A light rain was falling. Shrouded in darkness, the burned plains of the crumbled city were still smoldering, red embers glowing here and there. Among the burning ashes, flickers of distinctly blue flame would hover momentarily in the air before dropping back to earth. *Ghost lights!* I thought, certain that they were radiating from dead bodies lying there.

We waited in the dark, deserted station until after midnight before we finally managed to board a train. Many times, at the sounding of an air-raid siren, we were made to disembark and herded into nearby bomb shelters. Overcome with exhaustion, we thought we'd rather die than have to move again.

Meanwhile, father, bearing my brother's dead body, had traversed the hills and was walking along a narrow path through broad fields when he came under machine-gun fire from an American warplane. With no place to hide, nor any inclination to flee, he continued silently on his way, pulling the cart with Hideo in it behind him. The plane circled several times, aiming at my father, then flew off.

My brother Hideo was born while my father was in China as an army civilian. No sooner had father arrived home than he was sent back to China again, this time to work in a company in Manchuria. One year before the bomb was dropped, he was repatriated after his sciatica started playing up. And so it was that he and Hideo had very little time together as father and son. On fine days, father would take Hideo down to the river almost daily to go fishing and the like. If it were cloudy or rainy, he would carve small boats from wood, connecting engines to some, and float them in the bathtub with Hideo.

Engrossed in play with his young son, he would almost forget the time of day. Naturally Hideo loved his father and used to run after him in tears, whenever he went out.

On the morning of August, the sixth, they exchanged the following conversation:

"Dad, please take me with you."

"But you have school today, don't you? I'll take you with me next time, okay?"

"That's a promise, right?"

These were to be the last real words they spoke to each other.

I wonder what went through father's mind when targeted by a warplane as he walked alone through the fields bearing my brother's dead body.

Thanks to my father, who was uninjured – or at least had no major injuries – my immediate family and grandmother's household were all reunited. Faced with no food, nor any hope of receiving medical treatment for our wounds, we clung together to survive, but the mainstay of our two combined households – twelve members in all – were my uninjured father and grandmother, who was likewise unscathed.

Once some semblance of normalcy began to return, father took on community work as well. He was so good natured, people used to call him 'Saint Kaneyuki'. But he had no waged work. Of course, he wasn't the only father without a job in those days.

The night before my first day at work, my father sat me down before him and gave me the following three instructions:

"You mustn't judge people based on wealth or position."

"In terms of ideology, I hope you will follow the center and not lean to the extreme right or left."

"In matters of love, you are free to make your own decisions. However, marrying is about bearing descendants for the family. My wish is that you will carry on our blood line."

I wanted to question my father on the last of these three instructions but was silenced by his unusually solemn words. That was the only time I ever received any moral instruction from my father. Leaving the third principle aside, the first two principles are fundamental to my philosophy, and although I've never said anything to them as such, I feel that my three sons have likewise inherited these convictions.

# My Father, Masao

My father, Kaneyuki Masao, was philosophical about life, accepting whatever came his way. Father's grandfather, Kaneyuki Magoshirō, relinquished his right to inherit the family estate. Then his father Kaneyuki Jūtarō went bankrupt and had to close his judo center, leaving the family destitute. Father left school after graduating from upper primary,[10] and went to work to support his younger brother and sister through teachers' college. He said that in those days, in rural Japan, boys commonly quit school and went out to work after finishing lower primary with less than a handful each year going on to upper primary.

There was a certain stonemason father had admired from the time he was just a young boy. The mason was similarly fond of father and as time passed, came to treat him like a son. Father looked up to him as a master; indeed, he followed him into the trade, travelling the country under the mason's tutelage. Father also went to central China with the Japanese army, at one stage as a conscripted soldier, another time as a civilian employee. Not long before the end of the war, he was working in Manchuria. Then, after the atomic blast, he worked for Hiroshima City Council as a temporary employee, tending the gardens at Hiroshima Castle.

I was in fourth grade at primary school, as I recall, when we were given the task one day of finding out about our family crest and family tree for homework. When I asked father, he

---

[10] Upper primary was a four-year course that followed on from the compulsory, though not necessarily free, four-year lower primary education program. Children started school at seven.

said the family crest was the Paulownia emblem, *kiri*,[11] and that we could trace our ancestry back through the generations to Ōe Masafusa,[12] the Heian Period[13] scholar who provided academic and military training for the famous military commander, Minamoto Yoshiie.[14] This reminds me that the only book father ever gifted me as a little girl was the picture book, *Hachimantarō Yoshiie.*[15] The large, rather splendid book of illustrations must have been quite an expense when we were so poor. One of the pages of illustrations is still vivid in my mind's eye; it was of the episode where Masafusa detects poison in the sweet steamed buns presented as a gift to Hachimantarō.

Many, many generations later, long after the surname Ōe was changed to Kaneyuki, there was a dispute over inheritance rights resulting in a younger son, from a different bloodline, becoming the heir to the family. "In actual fact, we're the legitimate bloodline but his family took the family records," father said with a wry smile. The family that had assumed the family line was known locally as Kaneyuki *honke*, or 'the main branch' of the Kaneyuki family. They lived in a splendid house built, like a castle, on tall stone foundations. For some reason, whenever they went past, the village children would hold their breath, fold their thumbs into their palms 'in case they rot', and break into a run.

On display at my father's family home, in the large *doma* room with its traditional earthen floor, were a long spear and police lantern, while in the storage room upstairs, packed away in several black-lacquered chests, were various lacquered

---

[11] The *kiri* or Paulownia crest is the official emblem of the Prime Minister's office and used on official government documents. In earlier times, dating back to 12th century Japan, it seems that the imperial family used the Paulownia as a private seal before adopting the Chrysanthemum seal which is still used today as a symbol of the emperor and imperial family.

[12] Ōe Masafusa (1041–1111) was a well-known scholar and politician of the late Heian Period.

[13] Heian Period (794–1185)

[14] Minamoto Yoshiie (1039–1106)

[15] Hachimantarō was the name by which Minamoto Yoshiie was commonly known.

vessels inscribed with Kaneyuki Magoshirō – the name of my great grandfather.

One day when he was at junior high school, my brother Mikio said to father, "Everyone keeps calling me Kin-chan.[16] Are we of Korean descent?"

"The Japanese are a mixed race," father replied. "We're made up of ethnic groups immigrating from the north, including the Ainu and Caucasians from Russia, and immigrants from the south, the Chinese continent, Korea, and so forth. Our Korean lineage is one thing that appears to have been established beyond doubt." On another occasion he commented, "The reason why they don't excavate Emperor Nintoku's tomb is they're afraid of disclosing his Korean lineage. The Heike were descendants of Emperor Kammu[17] but they say that Kammu's mother's family immigrated from the Korean peninsula, possibly Paekche. On the other hand, the Genji commander, Minamoto Yoshimitsu[18] was commonly called Shinra Saburō, Shinra being written with the same Chinese characters as for the ancient Korean kingdom of Silla. My ancestors descend from Yoshimitsu's line. On the Korean Peninsula, Paekche and Silla were constantly at war with each other, while the Heike and Genji fought a long battle in Japan."[19] Father always said,

"Regardless of the imperial family's bloodline, we are a people of the Eurasian Continent, our culture came from the continent. China is the father, Korea the older brother, Japan the younger brother. That people of the same country, or the one planet, should engage in warfare against each other is the height of foolishness."

There was only one occasion when I was taken aback by his words. It was when I was seeking my first job. Evidently, the Bank of Japan customarily employed a graduate each year

[16] 'Kin' is the Sino-Japanese reading for 'kane', the first character in the surname Kaneyuki. It is also a common name in Korea.

[17] Emperor Kammu (737–806) reigned from 781 to 806.

[18] Minamoto Yoshimitsu (1045–1127) was the younger brother of Yoshiie. Like Yoshiie, he was a military commander.

[19] The Heiki and Genji were two powerful clans that fought a series of battles for ascendency in 12th century Japan.

from my high school, Hiroshima Girls High School of Commerce. On my teacher's recommendation, the bank offered me employment but I was averse to institutions, like banks, whose business was money; I rejected the offer. My teacher then recommended me to an American trading company. The pay was exceptionally good and I was interested in the future prospects presented by the job but when I discussed it with father, he spat out, "So you want to be used by the bastards who dropped the bomb!" At these unusually angry and scathing words, I immediately dropped the idea of joining the company.

On August sixth, the day of the blast, and the following day, August the seventh, father had trudged the entire city, from east to west, north to south, in search of me and other family members. He witnessed horrific scenes of devastation and suffering along the way; a city turned instantly to rubble, people – so disfigured they no longer seemed human – dead or dying amidst an unbelievable hell. A witness to such chaos and suffering and yet lacking the means to assist either on the day or for the many months and years that followed, had father harbored an intense anger, and contempt as a fellow human being, toward the country that dropped the atomic bomb on Japan? As I struggled to learn English conversation in my sixties, I often regretted not joining the American trading company.

After marriage, my husband and I moved to Kamakura. "Ah, what a wonderful day! I went to visit our ancestors' graves," father had exclaimed, his face beaming, the first time he visited us there. It was at dinner, the evening after his arrival. Midway up the hill behind the grave of Minamoto Yoritomo, [20] are two *yagura* tombs, [21] one belonging to the Shimazu Clan – descendants of the Minamoto,[22] the other the

---

[20] Minamoto Yoritomo (1147–1199): founder and first shogun, or military ruler, of the Kamakura Shogunate. He ruled Japan from 1192–1199.

[21] *Yagura* are man-made caves cut into the soft limestone hills around Kamakura and used as tombs and cenotaphs in the medieval period.

[22] The founder of the Shimazu Clan, Shimazu Tadahisa (d. 1227), was a son of the Shogun Minamoto Yoritomo (see note 20 above) and is buried in the tomb at Kamakura, near his father's grave.

resting place of Ōe Hiromoto,[23] the great grandson of Ōe Masafusa. Today, their tombs are tourist spots and there's a small plaque pointing the way, a far cry from when I moved to Kamakura over thirty years ago; then the dark, gloomy *yagura* caves merely gathered fallen leaves and dead branches dumped there – father did well to find the graves!

In our garden at Kamakura, sits a large mortar made from granite, said to be my father's very first creation as a mason. Father sent it to me from Hiroshima on the occasion of my third son's birth. He also made a wooden mallet for the children and taught them how to pound hot steamed rice to make New Year's rice cakes.[24] From then on it became a family tradition to pound steamed rice at the end of the year, a tradition that continues today even though my father is no longer with us. Once the children had outgrown the mallet, we split it into kindling and used it to cook the rice on a rice-pounding occasion, in remembrance of my father. Father also carved a stone lantern for each of my three sons, each with its own distinctive shape. I can still picture the look of bliss on father's face as he tapped at the stone with his chisel; he must have truly loved working with stone.

Father had made his first visit to Kamakura when my third son was in first grade at primary school; he especially doted on this, his youngest grandchild. "The youngest child is all the more adorable because their time with us is so short," father murmured as he placed him on his knee. He was almost certainly remembering my brother Hideo, a first-grader, like my son was at the time, when he died from the atomic blast.

With my graduation from girls' college came employment. In actual fact, I had wanted to study further and was determined to get into Hiroshima University, even if it meant preparing for the examinations on my own. I studied like crazy, focusing on Math and English. How I acquired the textbooks, I don't recall. With only one exercise book I used and re-used it by writing over the original penciled notes with firstly blue-colored, then

---

[23] Ōe Hiromoto (1148–1225): Hiromoto was a *kuge*, or court noble, who originally served at the Imperial Court in Kyoto before becoming a vassal of the Kamakura Shogunate.

[24] Traditionally eaten at New Year in Japan.

red-colored pencils. In our cramped home, I found that the best time for me to study was when I was taking a bath. Baths in those days were in round tubs, called *goemon-buro*, made of iron with a lid that also served as a platform to sit on while bathing. To economize on water, we would only half fill the bath, which left around a third of the bath dry once immersed. I would use the dry surface as an exercise book, dipping my finger into the water to write *kanji*, math equations and English on the side of the tub by way of study. The letters soon dried against the tub's warm surface and evaporated. The tub was thus a never-ending notebook, and the small bathroom, my own private study.

In 1946, the year after the atomic blast, the government devalued the yen in order to keep down inflation. Each household was given a limit of 500 yen per month to withdraw from their savings, the remainder was rendered valueless. We were now destitute. I nevertheless continued my solitary studies, unable to abandon this tiny ray of hope. The time came, however, when I inevitably had to give up the idea of going to university. Not breathing a word to my parents, I secretly burned my precious textbooks in the fire that heated the bath, shedding lonely tears.

I found employment at the Communications Bureau near home. I chose the Bureau not only because it was close but also because it had its own hospital right next door. My paltry wage was our family's only regular income. We all worked despite poor health but it grew harder and harder to make ends meet. When mother eventually collapsed, we convinced her that she needed to go to hospital. Though she was given medication, the doctors were unable to determine the precise nature of her condition. Several days passed and she still wasn't able to get out of bed; her condition grew steadily worse. It was then that we discovered that she hadn't been taking her medicine. "But what else am I to do? When the medicine runs out, you'll only have to go and buy some more for me..." she explained.

Despite these incredible hardships, *hibakusha*, [25] or survivors of the atomic bomb, received no assistance

---

[25] *Hibakusha*, literally 'explosion affected persons', is the term commonly used to refer to survivors of the atomic bombings.

whatsoever from the government. It wasn't until twelve years after the blast that the Hibakusha Medical Care Law[26] was instituted providing free medical care for blast victims. A great many people – how many in all? – must have lost their lives in the interim.

While still at junior high, my younger brother worked part time weaving bamboo strips for lath walls – slender strips of bamboo would be woven into a tight grid and used as the supporting frame for walls – a job that left his fingers on both hands cut and bleeding. Hidden in the leaves of my brother and sister's high school textbooks were numerous invoices from the school. They knew our parents couldn't afford to pay the school fees; not wanting to worry them they didn't pass them on. Eventually my sister quit school and took up a temporary position with the Ministry of Postal Services. "Mikio's a boy so he needs to at least finish high school," she explained.

Father suffered dreadfully from sciatica pain – some nights we would all lie awake listening to his groans – but he didn't let this deter him from clearing a patch of ground on the burned-out ruins of our home to make a vegetable garden and grow many varieties of vegetables for us. He also travelled back and forth to Saka where little by little he raised a plot of sweet potatoes which mother used at one stage to run a *yakiimo* baked sweet potato stall to help support the family. I used to go with father on Sundays to help. Watching him doggedly walk the two kilometers to the station, stopping to rest at the roadside every five or ten minutes on the way would bring tears to my eyes.

Never angry, nor known to grumble, father was a man of few words. Once we started getting the newspaper, he would spend several hours of the day reading the news. When he finished with the news articles, he would move on to the puzzles and quizzes – I don't doubt that he read every single

---

[26] For over a decade, no special provision was made for medical or economic relief of *hibakusha*. Only after an American nuclear test on Bikini Atoll in March 1954 that exposed and contaminated the Japanese fishing vessel and crew of Daigo Fukuryū Maru, did concerted efforts to introduce legislation in Japanese officialdom start.

word in the daily paper! And he was never one to be swept along by information from others, forming instead his own judgment based on what he had seen and considered. As a young man he travelled throughout Japan as a stonemason and even went overseas to work. There's a photo of him in the army uniform of a Senior Private but I never heard him speak of the war. After he married, he was sent to China as an army civilian.

One day when we were living in Saka, I spotted my father striding along the road toward me, smiling broadly. I will never forget that smile of his, or the bright, warm sunshine that day. That evening, as I lay awake in bed, I heard my parents talking in the living room, next to the room where I lay. "The Japanese soldiers did some dreadful things, you know…They'd capture a Chinese, tie his legs to a cow on either side then whack the cows' rumps so they would take off in opposite directions. They tore humans in half like that." I shuddered with fear, now more awake than ever. "And if they saw any women, they'd rape them, one after another."

"Did you do that too?" I heard my mother ask anxiously. "Absolutely not!"

Just as in the past he'd modeled wooden boats of various shapes and sizes from scraps of wood, filled the washbasin with water and enjoyed floating them in the basin with Hideo, father now made boats for my sons. Some of them were quite splendid with masts and coats of brightly colored paint.

Father used to repeat how his father, my grandfather Jūtarō, only taught him the art of self-defense because he claimed "Masao was too short tempered to be taught the full art of judo." One evening, we had been sitting around laughing and chatting when, pestered by my sons who were now at primary and junior high school, father headed with a chuckle down to the tatami room. "Alright, I'll show you how to revive someone who has passed out, but that's all!" I heard him say. The next moment, I heard loud thuds of people crashing to the floor. When I went to take a peek, I saw father standing in the stance of a true judo expert, challenging the children with the words, "Come on then, all three of you, try to attack me from wherever you like."

On another occasion when my father and children were chatting, I heard the children ask, "Ojiichan, have you ever had a fight?"

"Sure have."

"Are you strong?"

"Well, put it this way, I've never lost a fight. But then, I've never initiated a fight either, only taken up the challenge when provoked. On one occasion, a group of ten or so boys decided they were going to 'beat up Masao' and came spoiling for a fight. 'Okay,' I said, 'but on one condition; there's a team of you and only one of me so let me determine the time and place.'" Father chose a narrow street with a steep cliff on one side and a valley on the other for the venue, and for the time of day, sunset. No matter how many opponents there were, they could only attack him one at a time, and one-on-one, they were no match for father, who was not without some skills in the art of judo. Several of them came at him, the setting sun shining brightly in their eyes, only to be thrown, one after the other, to the ground. After that, it seems the would-be combatants fled.

Then there's the story about when mother and father married. Apparently, her mother-in-law said to mother, "You'd better watch your step as Masao has a short temper and is quick to use his fists!" When I queried father about this, he replied, "It's easier to hit your wife and children than it is to hit a cat; a cat can run away. It's not manly to hit things that can't flee. When I married, I resolved never to hit my wife or children." My father married my mother at thirty. She was the thirteenth woman introduced to him as a prospective marriage partner. "She was so beautiful," he would say, "like a heavenly maiden!" Perhaps it was indeed a heavenly maiden that changed my father.

Father had been working in Manchuria for several years before the end of the war. He returned home a year before the atomic blast, having injured his back. Later in life, he bought a TV and it seems that he used to watch the news and documentaries on it. If there was ever anything I wanted to know, I'd always ask my father. He knew everything, be it about Japan, the world, history, geography, or politics. I wasn't the only one to seek his advice; a youth in the neighborhood used to come to see my father too whenever he had any queries, doubts, or worries. "He's a sensitive, intelligent boy. I only hope he doesn't go off the rails, growing up as he is in such a difficult family environment," my father would say with concern. It seems father did what he could behind the scenes to support the boy. There were four children in the youth's family with only women – the mother and grandmother – to look after them. At times, they had to steal for food. The oldest daughter was one year younger than me; from the time she was fourteen or so she would draw the curtains in their shack and invite men inside. The neighbors looked down their noses at her, deeming her a 'loose woman', but looking back, it seems to me that she almost certainly did it to support the family. The youth ended up leading a sad life, just as father feared.

The atomic bomb destroyed people and their lives like this.

On the evening of 30th December, 1986, father slipped and fell when climbing out of the bath. He split his skull and lost a lot of blood. He went to see the doctor at the local medical center, whom my parents thought of as their family doctor, but the center had closed its doors for the year, and the doctor, having consumed a number of drinks over dinner, was well and truly inebriated. A former surgeon, he sewed up the opening, gave father first-aid treatment then sent him home. Father was never one to let injuries get the better of him, and sure enough, several days later, the wound had healed. But from around that time, he lost his power of speech and movement in his hands. Concerned, my mother took him to see a doctor she knew at a larger hospital and had him hospitalized. It was arranged for him to have a CT scan after New Year but it was too late, the hemorrhaging was beyond treatment by then.

On January the 8th, at the age of 89, father's hard life came to an end. After his death, we learned that he had colon cancer and had so for several years. In those days, cancer was considered fatal and most doctors tended not to tell the patient, or the patient's family.

Our family doctor was one such doctor.

Father lived an honest, poverty-stricken life. He left all the worries about how to make ends meet to mother. Apparently, his last words to her were 'thank you!'

# My Older Sister, Mitsuko

My older sister, Mitsuko was raised by our maternal grandmother Kiku, in the Doi family home. On the morning of the blast, she was in the kitchen at grandmother's house and saw its brilliant flash. In the intensely bright light, she said she saw every single particle of the garden's sandy soil rise up into the air. The next thing she knew, she was lying under the kitchen sink of the Murai's house next door. She must have been blasted through the walls and across the pathway between both houses. Walls in those days were made from multiple layers of clay – at least four – plastered over a gridded framework of bamboo lathes. It was impossible to break through such walls, especially the bamboo lathes, without the help of a sharp bladed instrument. So many people caught under collapsed houses couldn't be saved the day of the blast; those lath walls, for one, must have hindered their rescue.

How was it possible for my sister to have been hurled through the lath walls of both houses? Many strange things happened in those split seconds following the explosion. In my case, I had been standing by the window at the Savings Bureau when, the next minute, I found myself crouched at the foot of a large pillar in the center of the room. In addition to the usual staff desks and chairs, the area between the pillar and the window had been furnished with office equipment and several large bookshelves.

My sister managed to crawl out from under the ruins but her face was badly wounded, especially around the eyes, and bleeding heavily. "Help! Matsuko and Masakatsu are buried under here," she heard grandmother scream. Wiping away the blood, she started in the direction of her cries when Mr. Murai called her back.

"Mitchan, lend me a hand, will you? I can help too once I'm freed." She saw that his legs were sandwiched between a pillar and planks of wood; she helped free him and together they rushed to grandmother's aid just as Aunt Tomiko, who had been on her way to work when the bomb exploded, arrived back home. Mother and Aunt Hatsuyo also came running.

Together, they finally managed to free Matsuko and her baby, just as the fires closed in.

Mitsuko is in fact my half-sister fathered by another man, and goes by the surname Tanaka. My mother, Haruko, was the second daughter of Doi Yoneichirō and his wife Kiku. The Doi's were poor with many children; mother told of how she used to go to Hakushima Primary as a little girl with her youngest brother strapped on her back. Her father, Yoneichirō, had two younger sisters, Sue and Yuha. Sue married Fujita Ichirō, the founding president of the Fujita-gumi company.[27] At the time they married, he was still only an employee at a timber company but eventually he left to set up his own business. During his time as president of Fujita-gumi, he grew the company enormously, expanding it overseas as well. Our home after the blast – a tiny A-frame hut that made people green with envy – was a gift from the company.

Yoneichirō's other sister, Yuha, married Honda Gonpei, the son of one of Hiroshima's rich and illustrious families that owned a brokerage company. My mother used to tell us how as a teenager she was sent to live with the Honda's for a time in order to learn proper etiquette. She described life with the Honda family as like living in a lord's manor. It was her task to serve her uncle who took his evening meal in the family drawing room at the rear of the house. He would be seated before a small, low tray table, with his back facing the *tokonoma* alcove.[28] Aunt Yuha was very elegant and beautiful, looking just as if she'd stepped out of one of those traditional Japanese paintings of female beauties. Being steeped in

---

[27] Present day Fujita Corporation.

[28] The *tokonoma* is the small, slightly raised, alcove in a traditional Japanese drawing room. It is the focal point of the room, typically decorated with calligraphy or a picture scroll, and a flower arrangement.

traditional protocol, she always had dinner in another room with her maids. During her stay at the Honda's, mother learned tea ceremony, the art of flower arrangement, and how to play the *koto*.

Aunt Yuha and Uncle Gonpei were childless. In the evenings, Uncle Gonpei would visit his mistress. Every night when, at the designated hour, the regular rickshaw driver arrived to pick him up, Aunt Yuha would see him off at the entrance, where she would kneel down, delicately pressing the first three fingers of both hands to the floor and bowing her head down low to meet them. Aunt Yuha was the aunt I had gone to see on the day of the blast while Yoshiaki waited for me at Miyuki Bridge. She had informed me of how my family had fared.

At Uncle Gonpei's company was a promising young businessman by the name of Tanaka Toyosaku. Uncle Gonpei valued him greatly, treating him like his right-hand man. Aunt Yuha also doted on him. Eventually, Toyosaku and mother fell in love. They received everyone's blessings and were given a magnificent wedding ceremony – my mother, the lucky bride at nineteen! The following year, Mitsuko, my mother's eldest daughter, was born. But good fortune was to be short lived as not long after Toyosaku came down with typhoid fever and passed away within days of being hospitalized; heartbroken, mother returned with baby Mitsuko to her family home.

The Doi family was a large one. When the oldest son, Torao, married, bringing his young bride into the family home to live, mother had no choice but to leave her daughter in grandmother's care and remarry. She married my father, Kaneyuki Masao, when she was twenty-three years old. It was an arranged marriage and they had only exchanged each other's photographs. At the wedding mother said that she thought, *so the man at my side is to be my husband*, but she was unable to turn to look at him.

The Kaneyuki family lived in a small coastal town, a thirty-minute train ride from Hiroshima on the Kure Line. My paternal grandmother, Fusa, apparently promised that while Masao might be the eldest son, if they married she would set him up in business, in a stylish shop selling small accoutrement for instance, and that once they had settled down, mother would be able to take charge of Mitsuko again but these were nothing but empty words. As the wife of the eldest son in a strongly patriarchal society, mother was obliged to tend to the daily needs of his large family while also helping on the farm. Mitsuko remained in her grandparents' care. The adults in the Doi family home showered Mitsuko with love and affection so she had a rather spoiled upbringing. Nonetheless, as she grew, she came to hate her mother for 'abandoning' her and resent my father for 'robbing' her of her mother.

My sister started work when she was fifteen at the Telephone Bureau but was working at the Communications Bureau near home at the time of the blast, after having been transferred there. She was fair skinned and pretty, like a gorgeous Hakata doll. [29] This, and her bubbly, outgoing temperament meant she was immensely popular among the young men, who fawned over their 'Mitchan'. When I joined the Communications Bureau several years later, everyone took one look at my pale complexion, pigtails, and somber attire, and observing my retiring personality, was evidently surprised. "What, is she really Mitchan's sister? But she's just like a nun!" they buzzed.

My sister was nineteen, at the height of her beauty, when the atomic bomb was dropped leaving her with ghastly facial injuries as mentioned earlier. The area around both eyes was particularly badly wounded and she was left with large dark scars even after treatment. "Plastic surgery will help disguise the scars," the doctor told her some years later, encouraging her to undergo further surgery but grandmother, who was like a mother to her, advised her against having any more facial operations. "You should be thankful that you didn't end up blind," she declared. My sister followed her advice yet every

---

[29] The Hakata dolls, or *hakata ningyō* take their name from the Hakata region, now part of Fukuoka city, in the southern island of Kyushu. They are a biscuit-fired ceramic doll, known for their gracefulness and elegant realism. They attracted world-wide attention after three artisans won gold and silver awards at the 1925 International Exposition of Modern Industrial and Decorative Arts in Paris and became popular overseas after World War II, when American soldiers took them home to the States as souvenirs.

time she met the remark, "Miss, you have black ink on your face," she would feel angry and unfairly treated by life, and gradually she became more and more resentful. "They should drop atomic bombs all over Japan, no, all over the world, then people will understand my suffering," she would say. And at the sight of me campaigning hard for the anti-nuclear movement, she would take me to task for 'meddling'. "Think you can change the world, do you? What arrogance!" she would storm. Or she would slam me with the words, "You were able to live with your real parents, you'll never understand my suffering." There was no end to her grievances: abandoned by her mother, bomb injuries, no education. "No one has suffered as much as I have," she would say, "but I'm not going to let people get the better of me."

As I recall, she was in her mid-forties when she transferred to a private telecommunications company, at the recommendation of her former boss at the Postal Services Bureau (formerly the Communications Bureau). She was given an accounting position for which she had little experience but she studied and worked hard at the role, eventually earning everyone's complete trust. What drove her was this complex about not having had an education, and a stubborn refusal to let anyone get the better of her. In an age when it was rare for women to go out into the workforce, she became a manager, overseeing the company finances. Self-centered and proud by nature, her workmates used to humor her by calling her 'Her Royal Highness, Mitsuko', after Princess Michiko, wife of the prince and future emperor Akihito – a title that gave her much pleasure. Knowing her temperament only too well, no one in our family dared to go against her but it must have greatly pained my mother to be censured by her time and again for supposedly abandoning her.

Despite professing to have many admirers, my sister remained single, a fact that I find puzzling given that she had always wanted to marry. And although she never lived with us, she constantly tried to rule my life, which I found very tiresome as we are rather like chalk and cheese. But I was aware that my mother suffered most. "I don't understand why she turned out like this when her father Toyosaku was such a nice person," she would mutter.

Mother lived with my family in her later life. When my sister was 73 years old, and I was 68, mother collapsed from a stroke and passed away after only two nights in hospital. My sister criticized me harshly for crying over mother's sudden death. "Lay off with the sentimental tears, will you! Personally, I feel relieved," she chided, her eyes devoid of tears. I realized then that mother's death had freed my sister from the ambivalent feelings– a mixture of love and hatred – that she felt toward our mother and that had troubled her for so long. As a result, mother's death fostered a new sisterly bond between us. "Mother found happiness in her old age, thanks to you Fumiko," my sister would declare whenever we met up. "I'll be at a loss if you die before me; you're the only one I can rely on. You know that I'll be leaving you all my assets."

Everyone was poor in Hiroshima after the atomic bombing but the Doi family and my immediate family, who were born and raised there, were truly destitute, what with every member of the Doi household injured as a result of the blast, and their having lost their breadwinner, and then my father having to leave his job because of ill health. We managed to survive those difficult times by supporting each other, and perhaps because of that we all valued love over money. Everyone except my older sister, that is. She worshiped money. "Having no money is akin to being headless," she would say. She retired at sixty-three and with the onset of dementia, would hide her savings book and money here and there about the house where she lived alone, and then forget where she'd hidden them. And so she would spend her days hunting the house for them, hiding them in some other place whenever she found them, only to forget once again where she'd put them.

She is now eighty-seven years old and living in a retirement village in Osaka, where she has spent over half her life after leaving Hiroshima in her twenties. I heard that when she first entered the village, she used to rebel against the manager, packing up her belongings in a fury and declaring, "I'm going home!" But she's like a different person now and is well adjusted to, and content with life there.

My sister used to dote on my sons, totally spoiling them. They all visit her, my second son, who lives in Nara, goes every month, my eldest, in Kanagawa, twice a year – and of course I regularly travel down from Tokyo to see her – but she no longer recognizes them. Sometimes I give her a phone call. "You're the only one I recognize," I'll hear her declare at the other end of the line. "Why don't we go away on a trip together? Don't worry about the cost, I'll pay," she will say. "And when you make a trip home to Hiroshima, I want to go with you. I'll foot the bill, of course."

Whenever I go to Osaka to visit my sister at the retirement village, I stay in her apartment for several weeks and attend to her household affairs while I'm there. I feel her presence, especially when in the kitchen, and memories of when she was well and still living there come flooding back, filling me with sorrow. "I had no money when I first came to Osaka. See this frypan, I bought it for 150 yen!" "These are the curtains I bought with you in Tokyo. An unusual pattern, I know, but I love these psychedelic designs." On a recent visit she said with a smile, "I never forget your face!" I spent three or four hours reminiscing with her and was preparing to go when she suddenly enquired, as if she'd just remembered, "By the way, how's mother doing? It's such a long time since I last saw her. I've almost forgotten what she looks like!"

I constantly worry about dying and leaving Mitsuko. If there is such a thing as paradise, I hope the three of us, my mother, sister, and I, can spend happy times there together.

# My Younger Sister, Shizuko

My sister Shizuko was nine years old, five years my junior, at the time of the blast. She wasn't directly exposed to the fallout from the bomb as she was at a temple in the countryside where she had been evacuated with my younger brother Mikio, cousin Masaharu, and a large number of other school children under the government evacuation scheme. Nevertheless, she suffered from internal exposure to radiation as a result of our subsequent life on Hiroshima's burned-out plains. [30]

When she was little, Shizuko was a quiet, rather dull child but she grew into a lively, intelligent young woman. At the time when we were faced with extreme poverty, knowing how important it was for her older brother, as a male, to continue his studies, she made up her mind to leave high school and found work as a temporary typist at the Ministry of Postal Services. You could always hear her singing as she helped with the housework in the mornings before leaving for work, and again in the evenings on her return.

One day she brought home a large cup after winning the Prefecture's annual typist competition. The regulations stated that you could keep the cup if you won it three years in a row. I'd won the cup the previous two years but hadn't taken part that year because I was in hospital in Tokyo at the time, receiving treatment for my strange illness. "If only you'd won Fumiko, we could have kept the cup for good!" my sister said with some regret.

I was in and out of hospital every year, returning to Hiroshima when my symptoms improved only to find they

---

[30] Secondary or internal radiation exposure refers to exposure to radiation through ingesting tainted food or inhaling dust containing radioactive materials.

worsened almost immediately and I was back in hospital. Once hospitalized, I normally spent a good six months there. One day I received a telegram saying that Shizuko was in a critical condition. I dashed back to Hiroshima on the night train but she died before my arrival. The official cause of death was given as peritonitis and pneumonia but in reality, she had taken her own life. In one of my drawers I discovered an empty bottle of sleeping pills and a folded note with the words, "Short is the life of a flower, many are the troubles that afflict us."[31] She was just nineteen years old.

I suspect that Shizuko wouldn't have died had I been at home. Unwell – looking back, they suffered from terrible radiation afflictions – and destitute, father and mother toiled daily to support the family. Meanwhile, Mikio, for whom my sister had sacrificed her own education, was drinking heavily. I was the only one she felt she could rely on but I was in hospital with an intractable disease, said to be fatal. Indeed, at the time that she most needed me, I was fighting for my life after an adverse reaction to an Adrenocorticotropic hormone (ACTH) injection given to stimulate my adrenal cortex hormones. That must have been the final blow for her. "She'd never have died had you been here," blurted out mother who grieved for her day and night. Guilt weighed heavily on my heart.

Large numbers of people from Shizuko's workplace attended the funeral, including her boss, many of her colleagues, and even workers from the other divisions, a fact that surprised us but also made our grief all the more difficult to bear. Several days later, one of her colleagues visited and tearfully told us that Shizuko had been relentlessly bullied by one of the senior typists who apparently envied her, not only because she was so well-thought-of and trusted by all the bosses, but also because she'd had the audacity to win the typist's cup when she was only a temporary typist and 'high school drop-out'. On what turned out to be her last day at work, Shizuko evidently walked off in the opposite direction from home as they all left work. "Don't tell me you're going to the

---

[31] A well-known poem by poet and novelist, Hayashi Fumiko (1903–51)

74

drugstore to get some sleeping pills," the jealous colleague had jeered after her.

Let me briefly discuss the colleague in question. Hiroshima Communications Bureau was close to home and had its own hospital right next door, which is why I chose to work there after the war, being prone to illness at the time. I was assigned to the documents division in the secretarial section, where I began work while also undergoing training as a typist. I think there were around four sixteen-year-olds, myself included, among the new employees the year I started. We were each assigned a more senior employee to show us the ropes. The new entrant at the desk next to mine was inducted by the senior employee or colleague said to have bullied Shizuko. She was greatly admired by the newcomers for her kind and considerate teaching approach.

The year after I joined the Bureau it was split into two different entities, Japan Post (currently JP), and Japan Telecommunications and Telephone (currently NTT). Four of the younger employees, including me, were transferred to NTT, while the more senior staff nominated to be transferred to JP. The Bureau was housed in a stately building with a distinctive L-shape. The day after the blast, as seriously injured I made my way across the city that lay in rubble, my heart had leaped with joy at the sight of the L-shaped building in the distance signaling that I'd finally made it home. After the split, it was determined that the right wing of the building be used by JP, the left by NTT.

My sister Shizuko joined JP in the left wing. I heard that the kindly colleague whom the new entrants so admired would be teaching her the basics of typewriting, and when I saw her, thanked her for looking after my sister. "You must have noticed that X didn't attend the funeral? I bet she couldn't bring herself to," Shizuko's close colleague had commented. I had indeed been puzzled by her absence. I wished to meet her but strangely enough, I never again caught sight of her after that, even though we were both working in the same wing after I was discharged from hospital and returned to work.

On the day of the funeral something very mysterious happened. After the atomic bomb was dropped, mother arranged for a Buddhist priest to visit our home on the seventh of every month, to recite some prayers for my younger brother Hideo who had died in the blast. The priest was poor and always came attired in shabby old robes. Shizuko was filled with loathing for the priest, describing how on one occasion when mother briefly left the room during prayers, he had stretched out his hand to finger the food laid at the family altar as an offering to Hideo. I expect he was starving hungry. Never one to pass judgment on others, this priest was the only person about whom Shizuko voiced a strong dislike.

Receiving notice of the funeral, the priest set off along his familiar route to our home. Coming within a short distance of our house, however, he became disoriented and wandered up and down the street, unable to locate us. The service should have started and still he hadn't arrived. Large numbers of people had come to pay their last respects to Shizuko. A crowd formed in front of our house, spilling out into the street and stretching along the road into the neighboring street. A neighbor ran to call the head priest – a high-ranking priest and a fine specimen of a man – at nearby Mangyō-ji Temple. Eventually, our regular priest turned up but only after the hearse had already left. As usual he cut a poor figure with his weary expression and threadbare robes. "Wasn't it great that the priest from Mangyō-ji Temple came…and all those crowds of people!" murmured mother. "I'm so glad we were able to get that fine Mangyō-ji priest."

Shizuko had a bird's eye view of the temple from her office window. "Mangyō-ji Temple has a very nice graveyard, doesn't it? Every single grave is adorned with beautiful seasonal flowers…I've never seen any dead flowers lying around," she had once commented. When she was finding life difficult, I'm sure she must have gazed out the window at the temple's beautiful graveyard below and found some solace there. After Shizuko's death, father moved the family grave in Saka to Mangyō-ji Temple and cut a gravestone for her himself, positioning it so that it faced the window where her desk had been. Whenever mother and I visited her grave, we would always stop to gaze up at that window and reflect for a while.

In recent years, whenever I go home to Hiroshima, I meet up with Nishioka Seigo, a childhood friend and survivor of the bomb. One day we were strolling through the city when he remarked, "I once had a date with Shizu-chan at this café on the second floor. We left home separately and met up on the way....she was my first love!"

"Ah," I said, "So Shizuko experienced romance. Thank you for telling me!"

That was how I discovered that, though her life had been short and full of suffering, as a young woman, my sister had experienced the flowering, and breathed in the soft, sweet fragrance of love.

# Grandmother Doi

One person I must write about is my maternal grandmother, Doi Kiku. There is not a great deal to say about her experiences of the atomic bomb, however, as she spoke very little of those times.

At the time of the blast, grandmother was in the garden hanging out washing. When a blinding light fell on her face, she dashed up the steps onto the veranda in surprise. No sooner had she done so than the house collapsed around her. She managed to crawl out from under the ruins but her daughter-in-law, Matsuko, who had been feeding her baby rice gruel in the drawing room (apparently, Matsuko couldn't produce any breast milk at the time – the effect, perhaps, of malnutrition – and would mash rice gruel into a watery pulp to feed her baby), was trapped under the house with the baby.

When mother and Aunt Hatsuyo rushed over, grandmother pointed to a section of the collapsed house and screamed, "Masako and Masakatsu are under there, please hurry and dig them out!" This was no simple matter as the next-door neighbor's two-story home had collapsed on top of the house. What's more, they couldn't detect the baby's cries. Had grandmother not kept pointing and screaming frantically, "Matsuko and Masakatsu are under here," it's unlikely that the pair would have been saved. The fires had already reached them by the time they pulled them free. They all hastily fled to the river. "How is it that we ran across all that rubble in bare feet and yet never received any injuries?" they would marvel whenever the events of that day were recalled.

Life after the bombing was extremely hard, especially for my grandmother and her household. They suffered greatly from the tragic loss of Uncle Torao, their breadwinner, and each of them trod a harsh road through life after that. After the blast, grandmother's and my family's huts were built side by side with a shared kitchen area under the same roof much as if they were the one home – this was what my grandmother had expressly requested, having lost the support of Uncle Torao, her eldest son.

I must have spent a fair amount of my time doing tasks with grandmother when we were living in the huts. I was drying scraps of wood on the roadside with grandmother for instance when Miyo's father came seeking news of his family. And when he returned in the evening with a small container and said to her, "These are Miyo's ashes," I was again with grandmother, busy at some task outside our huts. We spent a lot of time those days gathering charcoal and scraps of wood that had survived the inferno, and drying them in the sun. We often came across bones as we worked, dry human bones, lighter even than the charcoal.

One day, grandmother and I were laying out scraps of wood and charcoal on the road to dry as usual, when a soldier with a large rucksack on his back approached us. It was early in the morning, as I recall, not long after sunrise. "Is this West Hakushima?" he enquired.

Grandmother stopped what she was doing before replying, "Yes, that's correct. Who is it that you are looking for?" He hesitated a moment then said,

"Ah, don't worry, I can't recall whether they lived at number four or number seven…"

"Are you trying to locate family? I know most people in Hakushima."

"Thank you but I think I'll just take a bit of a stroll around," he replied smiling shyly, then left.

"I expect he's another one who has lost all his family," I heard grandmother remark as I watched him depart looking sad and dejected.

In the evening on my way back home from an errand, I saw a dark figure trudging toward me, head bent. It was the soldier we'd seen in the morning. "Did you not manage to find the person you were looking for? This is East Hakushima, West Hakushima's over there," I said, offering to help him search once more but he shook his head sadly and said,

"It's no use, I'm going home." He looked crestfallen and thoroughly exhausted. I pointed out the way to the station although there was really no need, the road headed straight there across the burned fields.

The soldiers being repatriated to Hiroshima – now nothing more than an expanse of rubble dotted with shacks – had a sad aura about them, sadder even than the people living on the burned plains. There was a soldier I secretly kept an eye out for every time a new trainload came in. Toward the end of the war, I had inserted a postcard in an *imon-bukuro*, or 'consolation' parcel,[32] that mother had prepared for sending to a soldier at the front. There was no guarantee that the parcel would get through as American submarines had virtually blocked off all of the sea routes. Little domestic mail was getting through either; people were in an uproar over the prospect of a decisive battle being fought on Japanese soil, and women and the elderly were being rounded up into groups and given training on how to use bamboo spears. Then one day, a letter from a soldier arrived for me, having travelled all the way across the East China Sea from the distant battlefields. It came with a photo of a young soldier smiling in a field of flowers. "Crawling along the ground as bombs rain down on us, my eyes suddenly catch sight of beautiful wild flowers and I am momentarily transported away from the battlefield," it said. "It's evening and I'm in an army field tent. It's a beautiful moonlit night, the land, a vast, silent expanse. My army fellows and I have been savoring this brief interlude of peace and quiet while sharing a cup of sake and the one cigarette. I sang 'The Blue-Eyed Doll'.[33] Tomorrow, we'll be back under fire."

---

[32] Neighborhoods were responsible for organizing parcels for sending to soldiers fighting at the front.

[33] A children's song that became a popular hit in the 1920s when it was created (cf. 1921). Lyrics, Noguchi Ujō (1882–1945); music, Motoori Nagayo (1885–1945). The song predates, and should therefore not be confused with, the thousands (over 12,000) of 'American Blue-Eyed Dolls' that were sent to Japan in 1927 under a goodwill and friendship program initiated by the American missionary Sidney Gulick (1860–1945) as a way to ease growing tensions between Japan and America. Deemed an 'enemy song', singing 'The Blue-Eyed Doll' was banned during WWII.

Not long after that the atomic bombs were dropped on Hiroshima and Nagasaki, and Japan declared defeat.

One day, grandmother received a letter. Imagine! Our very first since the blast, the city having been cut off from all news from outside. There was no street address, only the place-name 'Hakushima' on the envelope. But it was addressed to me. "Not knowing where to find you, I searched all over East and West Hakushima, checking each and every shack time and again," it read. "As evening fell, I ran into a young woman who kindly informed me that I was in East Hakushima. "West Hakushima is over there," she said. I hope you are alive and well, like that young woman, and that you get to read this letter. I received well wishes from you when I was at the front, now it's my turn to pray for you, that you are still alive and, if you are, that you can survive without harboring a grudge or becoming cynical toward the world. If you do happen to receive this letter, please drop me a line."

After I replied to his letter, the young man often came to visit, a rucksack packed with food on his back. He and grandmother seemed to hit it off, developing a mutual admiration. He was a kind, retiring person. Sometimes, when he slept over in our crowded little hut, he would sing 'The Blue-Eyed Doll' for me. But he never spoke of the war. "Alone in the remote countryside, my elderly mother waited patiently for my return to Japan," he told me, "but as soon as I arrived back, I left her and set off again determined to travel around the country on foot, chasing flowers like a honeybee. I wanted to convey to their kin the dying words of my army friends who were unable to return to their homeland after falling in battle in a foreign land." Grandmother wished for the two of us to marry and tried many times to persuade my mother and me but I had to work to provide our family with a regular income, paltry though it was, and I was in any case engaged in an arduous on-going battle with that intractable disease.

I used to see grandmother almost daily; before the war, her home, the Doi family home, was in the same neighborhood as us, then after the blast our huts stood side-by-side, and later we lived on opposite sides of the road from each other. Not once, however, did I hear her cry or complain. A petite woman, at less than 140 centimeters tall, she lived her life before the war as the wife of the eldest son of a patriarchal family, then after the war as a housewife, helping her daughter-in-law with the housework and raising the children. Above all, she was the main pillar of support for her family. Grandfather was handsome with a fine physique but he forever saw the world through rose-tinted glasses and evidently lacked in a strong sense of duty to provide for the family. It therefore fell on my grandmother from early in their marriage to work to support the family. If she ever spoke of these matters, it was always with an air of child-like innocence.

The year she passed away, the cherry blossom was especially beautiful. It was April 12th and the cherry trees had just come into full bloom when, much as if she had been waiting for that very day to arrive, my diminutive grandmother quietly departed for the heavens.

She was 103 years old.

# Grandfather Doi

My maternal grandfather's name was Doi Yoneichirō. He was tall and handsome with a wonderful physique and the commanding, dignified presence of a Kabuki[34] actor. And he was one of the world's greatest optimists! Throughout his working life he drifted from one job to another. The longest job he ever held down was when he worked at the public baths but even then he left most of the work to my grandmother, Kiku, while he pursued his hobbies from dawn to dusk.

Grandfather's greatest hobby was growing chrysanthemum. In the flowering season, my grandparents' large entrance would be crammed with pots of chrysanthemum, each with a single magnificent bloom,[35] requiring everyone to squeeze past to get into the drawing room. And in a shed at the rear of the garden – evidently the old storage shed – he kept a variety of birds. Then, on fine days, he often went fishing. The only fish he ever brought home were wrasse. He'd fill a large tub with water and

---

[34] Kabuki is one of Japan's three main classical theatres the origins of which can be traced back some four hundred years to the early Edo Period (1600–1868). It is still popular today, having survived Japan's rapid westernization in the Meiji Period (1868–1912) and a brief ban by the occupying forces in the early post-WWII period. In 2005, Kabuki was designated a 'UNESCO Intangible Cultural Heritage'. Leading actors are celebrities in Japan, often featuring on television and in film roles.

[35] The chrysanthemum has been cherished in Japan since ancient times. The flower features in many works of classical literature and art and is an emblem of the emperor and imperial family. Over the centuries, the Japanese people have developed many cultivation and display techniques for the chrysanthemum, the 'single-stem style' – one large bloom atop a long, slender stem – being one of them.

release them into it; such beautiful fish, they would glide through the clear water, their bodies sparkling with the many colors of the rainbow. We children would watch engrossed, totally oblivious to the passing of time, while grandfather looked on, his face beaming. Grandmother grumbled about wrasse having a soft, tasteless flesh and never served them up for dinner.

Unperturbed, grandfather would arrive home from fishing with the usual catch of wrasse.

Among his close friends was a chap called Mr. Kuma. The two of them loved the hustle and bustle of festivals where they would have loads of fun running stalls selling bananas, lemonade and soda water and the like. They would fill a large barrel with crushed ice to chill the lemonade, and when they got down to the bottom of the barrel, they would sell off the few remaining bottles by tossing in a pile of crushed ice and stirring it with a large stick, creating such a lively racket that the customers would flock around. And so it was that 'Yone-san' and 'Kuma-san' were somewhat celebrities. Grandfather was also known as the 'festival man'. There were many festivals back then; shrine festivals, *Obon*, [36] mid-summer festivals with fireworks... Although he couldn't play the drums, or sing and dance, no festival would begin until 'Yone-san' appeared. I must have inherited grandfather's genes because I am a true optimist and get itchy feet at the sound of the festival drums.

Grandfather had the rather unusual habit of undressing whenever he went to relieve his bowels; back then people wore traditional kimono, which are all in one piece. Whenever we found his kimono lying outside the toilet door, we knew we'd have to wait a while before we could use the toilet.

Grandfather rented a large plot of land near the riverbank and planted it out in flowers. All year round there would be a profusion of flowers in bloom. Growing among the flowers were a large fig and loquat tree, a goumi bush and Nanking cherry. A small shed also stood on the plot. As children, we often went to grandfather's field, me to enjoy the flowers, my younger brother and cousin with their eye on the fruit. Mother

---

[36] See note on page 135 in 'Bone Statue of Buddha'.

told me that grandfather used to sell flowers across the river in Yokogawa but he never brought the money home. And even when food became very scarce, he never grew any vegetables. "He never did anything for the family," mother would say with a sardonic smile. Despite his failings, he was liked by all.

When, after the blast, starvation was rife, we would boil up grasses and eat sweet potato vines extracted from plots vacated by the military. One day we heard along the grapevine that they were selling Eba[37] cakes, and travelled a considerable distance to buy some.

People also called them 'bran cakes', and they were indeed made from some sort of bran or millet. They weren't the least bit tasty, leaving a sharp aftertaste that would sting the throat, but they were filling. The only problem was that everyone who ate the cakes ended up constipated and, while it may have had nothing to do with the cakes, also developed parasites. The parasites were ghastly things, fat white worms in one's stool. Once they got a hold, a cluster of them would settle in the intestine, badly affecting bowel movements.

Next, we heard that in Yokogawa, a neighboring town just across the river from Hakushima, they were selling delicious cakes made from a type of edible seaweed. Certainly, these were far tastier than the bran cakes and suitably dark in color for cakes with seaweed as an ingredient. The only drawback was the grainy sand in them. And it was rumored that they were behind the large number of appendicitis cases at the time. Nevertheless, the cakes were so popular a line of people would form in front of the shop from early morning. The small, flat cakes of around seven centimeters in diameter were limited to four per person; some people dragged their babies and toddlers along, as they could be counted. Needless to say, every member of my family was among those lined up at daybreak. People from all over the neighborhood would form a long line in front of the shop – whether a small stall or a vending-cart, I don't recall. Some latecomers would try to jump the queue.

---

[37] Eba is the name of a district in Hiroshima. It lies near the mouth of the Ōta River, south of central Hiroshima and Bun's hometown, Hakushima, and at its southern-most end faces Hiroshima Port.

"Come now, what do you think you're doing?" my grandfather would drawl, at which they would drop back. On the way home, around Misasa Bridge, grandfather would succumb to the hunger pangs and munch on a cake. This would greatly anger my grandmother. "When we get home, these are to go into a large pot of water to boil up as soup to keep us fed for the day." The cakes were so small that, even had he demolished four of them, they would never have assuaged grandfather's hunger. Grandfather would reluctantly apologize but the next day the same thing would happen; we'd reach Misasa Bridge, he'd bite into a cake and grandmother would admonish him.

My family's greatest asset when we lived in our tiny A-frame hut was a large two-wheeled wagon. His younger sister being the wife of Fujita-gumi's company president, grandfather was able to procure materials from the company to build our huts as well as a wagon to transport them. When we weren't using the wagon, we would remove its wheels and deck, and lean them up against the broken-down fence of Hakushima Primary School. One day, a man started assembling the wagon on the side of the road; from all appearances, he intended to steal it. Grandfather and I followed the man's movements closely from inside the hut. He had finally managed to assemble the cart and was all set to run off with it in tow when, just at that moment, grandfather boomed, "Come now, where do you think you're going with that!" in his usual lazy drawl. The man looked around him in surprise then beat a hasty retreat.

"You don't mean to say that the pair of you were watching him the entire time as he assembled that wagon! You surely could have warned him earlier!" my mother said with a look of amazement.

Grandfather named his eldest son Torao, and his second son Kumao. When the third son came along, he said, "If we have a tiger and a bear, then we need a rock," and gave him the name Iwao.[38] Torao died from the atomic blast, Kumao and Iwao died from diseases.

---

[38] Torao, Kumao and Iwao derive respectively from tora, meaning 'tiger', kuma, meaning 'bear', and iwa, meaning 'stone'.

On August 6th, grandfather was at his plot, around 1.3 kilometers or so from the hypocenter. Although he was working outside, the fig tree or loquat must have shielded him from direct exposure to the rays from the blast as he came away with just a tiny burn, around the size of a ten-yen coin, on the back of his neck. But as the days passed, the burn spread down his neck and over his back. Exuding a foul odor, the wound became infested with maggots and gave off a greenish glow in the dark.[39]

Grandfather was forever laughing heartily, even when we lived in our small huts on the city's burned wastelands. Once life began to settle down, he would head down to the public baths every afternoon, although we had our own bath, and it became a favorite pastime of his to laugh and chat away the afternoon with his friends at the baths until evening came around. Over the years, one by one his group of friends gradually shrank, and in his later years, he appeared a rather lonely figure. He passed away on the 30th September, twelve years after the end of the war, after only a few days ill in bed. He was eighty-eight years old.

One day toward the end of his life, after he had fallen ill, he shouted, "Watch out, the water's coming!" and tried to scramble out of bed. His daughter-in-law, my Aunt Matsuko, hoisted him onto her back and walked around the room pretending to flee. His cries must have been brought on by the memory of the events of that September the year the atomic bomb was dropped; on September 17th, 1945, a fierce typhoon, the Makurazaki typhoon, hit Japan – according to the history records, 3,756 people went missing or were killed. We had only recently erected and settled into our huts. The two huts, one belonging to my grandparents, the other, my family's, had been built side-by-side on land a few meters above the road but the water rose up over the road and surged all around us, almost lifting our huts off the ground. It was a dark night. We all decided to evacuate to the Communications Bureau, except, that is, for grandfather who sat down inside saying, "I'm not fleeing anymore," and refused to budge. In the end,

---

[39] Although Bun doesn't provide details, her grandfather's injuries were no doubt left to heal naturally, like most others at the time.

grandmother forcibly dragged him out with her but when they stepped down to the road he fell and almost drowned. Then, just as we made it to the Communications Bureau, Aunt Matsuko suddenly disappeared under the water with the baby on her back; it seems she had accidentally stepped into a large ditch that ran alongside the Bureau. It was hard to wade through chest-high water in our weakened state, and in the dark, it was a desperate struggle to escape. None of us got any sleep that night; worried about our huts, we spent the night gazing out the dark windows. What a wonderful feeling it was when, in the faint light of dawn, we were able to make out our two huts.

Faced with death, grandfather must have recalled that terrifying night of the storm. Still, I'm sure that now, in heaven, he will be chatting cheerfully, even about such matters, with his buddies from the public baths.

# Uncle Torao

On the morning of the bombing, Uncle Torao, mother's older brother, went to the office as usual. The company where he worked was around three hundred meters from the hypocenter, off to the west of Hiroshima's main street. Not long after he arrived, there was a brilliant flash of light, followed by complete darkness. *A bomb's hit us*, he thought, sensing, in the dark, that the building had collapsed and that he was lying in a small clearing among the ruins. Gradually, the darkness faded and a shaft of light shone in.

"Doi-san, are you alright?" called out a colleague close by. "At any rate, let's get out. Follow me," the colleague said as he started making his way toward the light. Uncle crawled after him. Once outside, they realized that the entire city, and not just the company building, had been destroyed. Uncle was stunned. He felt numb. Meanwhile, he lost sight of his colleague.

Concerned about family, uncle decided, firstly, to head home. He started walking toward his home in Hakushima but soon lost his sense of direction amidst the devastation and vast expanse of rubble. Hiroshima lies on a delta, facing the sea to the south and surrounded by gentle undulating hills in the other three directions of the compass. Uncle had set off, guided by Mt. Futaba whose gentle lower slopes sweep out over north-eastern Hiroshima, but he evidently turned a little too far eastward and ended up at the military training grounds on Mt. Futaba's eastern foothills. That's where he met my father, as described earlier. Eventually reunited, he spent the night with family on the small island – locally known as Nakagawara – in the middle of the Ōta River, which flows around Chōjuen Park, enclosing it in its watery embrace.

On August the seventh, I had made my way across the city of death and by chance stumbled upon my mother, aunt, and sister. When we headed back to Nakagawara, we found that everyone had gone, apart from my uncle and grandmother who had stayed behind to inform us of the evacuation to Hesaka Primary School.

My uncle was a kind-hearted person – I can still see him in my mind's eye, a gentle smile spread across his face. Such a warm-hearted person and yet he was laid down on the concrete floor in a large, dingy room at the Communications Bureau, which had survived the fires, and left there without any treatment for the excruciating migraines which plagued him day and night. I will never forget the sight of his suffering. Mother and I visited uncle in that large room every day. So many injured lay on the floor, there was barely room to walk. I wonder, *did they receive any food or water?* We certainly never saw anyone receive any nourishment.

To get to where my uncle lay, we had to carefully pick our way through the gaps between the wounded who were so badly burned their skin would peel off at the slightest brush against them. Maggots infested their wounds and ate away at their raw flesh; the air was filled with their groans and the dreadful stench of rotting flesh. One after another they passed away. No sooner had the dead been taken away than their spot would be filled by another. While I never saw anyone receiving any food or drink, bandages would be applied to their wounds, becoming soaked almost immediately in blood and pus.

One day, as I sat beside my uncle, several nurses appeared and began changing people's bandages. The moans grew louder. As a layer of bandaging was removed, big fat maggots came tumbling out and started wriggling across the floor. With each unwinding, more and more maggots pattered like large drops of rain to the floor. For decades after, I would tremble at the sound of rain whenever there was a thunderstorm in summer, and cower at lightening which reminded me of the brilliant flash of light at the time of the atomic blast.

The person lying next to my uncle was wrapped from head to foot in bandages, only eyes, nose and mouth visible. Although I had seen many dreadful sights, I couldn't bear to watch when the nurses came to change this person's bandages; the moans – whether male or female, I know not – were horrific, while piles of maggots tumbled to the floor and crawled up my legs, no matter how many times I brushed them off. Next day, another of the wounded lay in their spot. In the midst of all this suffering, uncle, tended by my grandmother, bore his pain in silence, not wanting to further burden anyone. Whenever grandmother caught sight of what looked like a nurse, she would beg for some medication. "I'll get you some medicine soon," the nurse would say soothingly but uncle never did receive any. They likely had none to give. Uncle grew weaker and weaker. All we could do was look on in bewilderment as death crept closer and closer – we too were on the brink of death; at the time, none of us in the huts had any food or drink.

Uncle Torao's wife and young, seven-month-old son had evacuated to father's hometown along the Seto Inland Sea coast. "Shall we bring Masako and Masakatsu to see you?" grandmother and mother asked, aware that death was imminent, but uncle softly shook his head, "There's nowhere for them to sit here." And so it was that he passed away on August, 23$^{rd}$, without setting eyes on his wife or children. He was forty-two years old. My grandparents, and the other surviving members of our family, cremated his body on the charred grounds of Mangyō-ji Temple, around the corner from the Communications Bureau. His body didn't burn easily; time and again we had to go and gather scraps of wood from the burned-out fields to help relight the fire. *Uncle doesn't want to be cremated. He didn't want to die,* I thought and was filled with an unbearable sadness, breaking down in tears for the first time since the blast.

Next day, we went to gather uncle's bones. His brain matter had congealed into a hard, black mass. To the very end, Uncle had been kind and considerate toward those around him, never raising his voice or crying out, despite his suffering. Only yesterday he'd been alive, now he no longer existed. Never have I felt such a strong sense of transience and emptiness as I did at that moment. No doubt that was because, having lost all the trappings of life, and living on the vast burned-out plains, our lives, the mere fact of our existence, were all that we had.

Uncle's older son, my cousin Masaharu, had been evacuated with my brother, sister, and classmates to a temple in the countryside. After uncle died, Masaharu had been left in the temple's care as we were in no position to bring him back to Hiroshima. "Let's bring Masaharu back," father said one day and set off to collect him. "Can I really go home?" the young boy asked in delight before adding uneasily, "But why just me?" To the day that he died at 89, the memory of those events never failed to bring tears to father's eyes. For my part, I can still picture my cousin's thin, emaciated body as he sat with his back to us, clutching the small box containing his father's ashes, his head hanging dejectedly.

My uncle had been the main breadwinner for his large extended family. His death cast a long, dark shadow over the lives of the family members he left behind.

# Radiation Sickness

Following that initial violent attack on August 7th, the day after the atomic blast, I was never free from dysentery – which calls to mind our huts and the matter of toilets. My grandmother's family of seven, and my immediate family of five, built our huts side by side on Hiroshima's blackened plains, around the spot where we judged our houses to have originally stood. Mother's Uncle Ichirō, who ran the construction company, gave us the building materials. At one stage during the war, a hut made from the very same materials was put on display as a 'model hut' in front of the city council. It was a wooden, pyramid-shaped affair of around 12 *tatami* mats, or 20 or so square meters, in area, with a tar-sealed roof.

Transporting the building materials was an arduous ordeal that took several days. It must have been five or six kilometers from Hakushima to the warehouse near Miyuki Bridge where the materials were kept. The sun beat down on us and reflected off the rubble over which, injured and starving, we hauled our large, two-wheeled cart. The heat was unbearable; virtually naked, we could almost hear our skin sizzling in the sun. There was not a single tree for shade while the rubble threw off a sweltering heat but we had neither the time nor the presence of mind to think about resting. Several days later, we looked at each other and dissolved into laughter; against our gaunt and now deeply tanned faces, our eyes looked big and bulbous. "We can't get rid of the *pika*[40] tan, can we! We've all been dark

---

[40] *Pika* and *pikadon* are terms used by survivors to describe the atomic blast. Those who were close to the hypocenter at the time of the explosion tend to use the term *pika* (lit. 'brilliant light') as they only saw a brilliant light, while those who were slightly

skinned ever since," mother would often remark in years to come.

On the morning of August 7, I had parted with Yoshiaki at the foot of Miyuki Bridge and staggered northward across the city of death. Now we were travelling that same route, except this time we set out from the north and headed south before returning again with our cart in tow. Lying on the roadside en route was a horse's decaying corpse. Swarming in maggots, it gave off such a stench that we could smell it a mile off. Each time we came to the spot where it lay, we caught our breath and rushed past. Also along the way, where a liquor store had perhaps stood, was a heap of mangled glass bottles – they must have buckled and twisted in the heat from the blast. The sight of the bottles never failed to remind us of the enormous heat created by the atomic explosion and we would exclaim how lucky we were to have survived. The tall trees in Shukkeien Park were badly burned. Only a few branches remained, their black fingertips scratching against the sky – a strange sight that is still etched in my mind's eye.

Eventually, we managed to erect our A-frame huts with the brand-new planks we'd been given. Three huts in all, Grandmother's, my immediate family's, and a little further along, Aunt Hatsuyo's. Their triangular shapes stood out against the scorched, barren landscape and were clearly visible from afar. What a great source of envy they must have been for those living in makeshift shacks that they'd thrown together from scraps of corrugated iron and wooden posts scavenged from the burned remains of the city. Some people made a point of coming over for a closer look at our huts. "Fancy building such splendid houses!" they would exclaim loud enough for us to hear as they stood around gossiping. "Seems some people can afford to do so despite our losing the war!" On one occasion I was subjected to a diatribe, the jealous gossiper unaware that I was one of the huts' inhabitants. Having also been given some tatami mats from relatives whose home had survived the inferno, we really did have luxurious huts, worthy of people's envy.

---

further away also heard a loud boom (*don*) and therefore tend to use the expression *pikadon*.

There were seven living in my family's hut; me, my parents, my younger sister and brother who had returned from the temple in the countryside where they'd been evacuated, and the Murai's two daughters. Lacking materials to build a toilet, we decided to do our business behind Hakushima Primary School's partially collapsed fence. On reflection, it would seem that I may not have been the only one plagued with diarrhea for, although we ate little, everyone went to the toilet often. "Make sure you go well inside the grounds to do your business," grandfather would instruct but whenever I rushed in to go, more often than not I would find him squatting near the entrance. While we were hidden from view from our side of the fence, on the other side was a wide expanse of scorched fields that left us completely exposed.

One day, father turned up with some planks – goodness knows where he got them from – and built a toilet at the side of our hut. Several steps led up to the toilet. Inside was a boxed area with a round hole, top center, and that was all, but it had a long drop and a high ceiling and there was even a window so we were all greatly impressed when he finished. Next day, however, we went outside to find the toilet gone, lifted up by the wind in the night and blown some distance away. Although it had looked solid enough, father's amateur construction must have been unsound.

"What did you do for a toilet?" a fourth-grader asked me last year when I was giving a talk at a primary school.

"We hid behind the brick fence of a primary school which had survived the fires. We were out of view from our side of the fence but on the other side was nothing but a wide expanse of scorched fields so that we were visible for miles around."

"What did you wipe your bottoms with?" Unable to recall, I asked Aunt Tomiko next time we met at our family memorial service. "With grass…" she replied.

"But what about before the grass regrew?" In my mind's eye floated an image of white paper. To which she replied, as if she'd just remembered,

"As I recall, we found some paper in the burned-out remains of the old military headquarters built at the time of the

Sino-Japanese War[41] (I discuss the military headquarters in 'Children's World') and took it home where we used it sparingly for lighting fires and the like…" She then burst into laughter, adding, "Imagine, we wiped our bottoms with important military documents!"

I think it was in late summer, sometime after August 20th that our lives in the huts began. That autumn, I came down with a high fever. Mother would lay a wet towel on my forehead, and immediately steam would rise from it. Then, several days later, my gums swelled and began to bleed. I couldn't ingest any food or water and was wracked with pain all over. I felt as though I was disintegrating from within. Death seemed imminent. On the day of the blast, when I had been close to death, I felt no pain but this time I was in agony with the fever and swelling in my mouth. There was no medicine to be had at the hospitals, all one could do was lie down and rest. But what an amazing capacity humans have to survive! Before long I was up and about again and that autumn I had my first period – I sometimes wonder whether I really was menstruating or, more likely, bleeding as a result of radiation sickness.

As I recall, it was some six months after the blast when I first washed my hair. Everyone had burns and other injuries yet no one received any medical treatment; we were all left to heal naturally. I was covered in cuts from broken glass with an especially deep gash above my right ear. I filled a basin with warm water and lowered my head into it. Little by little I untangled my hair, which had turned as hard as a board after being soaked in blood from the wound above my ear, and washed the dirt away. Needless to say, we had no soap or shampoo. The first batch of hot water turned to a dirty grey slush, like mushy rotten seaweed, and gave off such a foul odor it made me shudder. I repeated the procedure, filling the basin many times, until I finally felt fresh and clean. Patting my head, it felt bald but there was no mirror to check.

At some stage, I'm not sure exactly when, survivors of the atomic blast starting having their blood tested at the Communications Bureau Hospital. All those lining up at the hospital had burns and lacerations. Dressed in rags and weak

----

[41] 1894

from starvation, they came, no doubt, with the expectation of receiving some medical care. But the hospital conducted blood tests and that was all. It was rumored that those with white cells numbering more than ten thousand or less than three thousand would die. Many of the survivors must have been sitting at around those numbers. I had roughly three thousand white blood cells; my mother was in the two thousands. After two or three visits, everyone stopped going to the hospital. What point was there when they provided no treatment for our injuries and merely syphoned blood from our already severely weakened bodies? Later, a large facility belonging to the United States army was built at the top of Mt. Hiji, a hill lying at the eastern end of Hiroshima City. This was run by the American army's 'Atomic Bomb Casualty Commission', commonly known as the ABCC, which likewise conducted blood tests and various other tests on the survivors of the blast. I discuss the ABCC in the next chapter.

After the atomic blast, mother often exclaimed, "Fumi-chan,[42] what on earth is the matter with you!" her eyes resting on me anxiously. Prior to the blast, I'd been 'the child with an amazing memory' but from that day on, it was much as if I had lost my mental faculties.

Though everyone was in a severe state of shock after the bombing, it seems that I was especially badly affected. Not only had my memory slipped, I went about my daily life as if in a daze and sometimes slipped in and out of consciousness. I had always been frail as a child and frequently had herpes attacks. After the blast, these attacks became so bad that I struggled to eat and talk even. I couldn't pronounce syllables beginning with 'm' for instance, where I had to bring my lips together. My lips were forever inflamed and would become glued shut if I didn't keep them slightly ajar. I dreaded going to sleep at night as in the morning I'd wake to find them caked together with dry blood and pus and would be reduced to tears in my attempt to part them. I tried using chopsticks and spoons to keep them apart as I slept but these invariably fell out during

---

[42] 'Chan', a term of endearment typically used for young girls, is here combined by Bun's mother with a shortened version of Bun's first name, Fumiko, again as a form of endearment.

the night. Once I tried gauze, with tragic results; everything became glued together, including the gauze.

In search of a cure, mother took me to every single hospital and medical center in the city. We even tried moxibustion[43] after seeing an advertisement in the newspaper. The doctor applied moxa to a hundred or so different spots on my body. My symptoms only worsened. I was 24 years old when they finally gave my illness a name; the intractable disease, Erythematodes.[44] Just around that time, antibiotic cortisone had come into use. This helped alleviate the symptoms of the disease that had by then been plaguing me for ten years. It had dangerous side-effects however; two young patients died while I was in hospital and needless to say, I too lived with the constant threat of death.

The Adrenocorticotropic hormone (ACTH) injection that I was once given shortly before I was due to be discharged from hospital, caused a shock reaction that brought me to the brink of death. It happened to be on the day the head physician was doing his regular weekly visit; the physician in charge of my case, various other doctors, and even some interns were all in tow. Just as the patient in the bed behind the curtain next to me was being examined, a small needle was inserted and its contents injected into my arm. About a minute later, my body started to go into a state of shock; the back of my throat began burning and felt as if it was about to burst, setting off a chain reaction that went through each of my internal organs. All of my body wastes were instantly discharged. I summoned up just enough strength to weakly call a nurse but after that lost the energy to speak or open my eyes even. Nevertheless, I could hear as the doctors and nurses crowded around my bed and rushed about shouting for 'Vitacampher', a medication used to prevent cardiac arrest. I was given several injections; each time

---

[43] Moxibustion is a traditional Japanese medical therapy originating in China. Dried, ground mugwort is applied directly to the skin of the patient, or used with acupuncture needles, and burned much like incense.

[44] An autoimmune disease that can affect the skin, joints, kidneys brain and other organs. See the final chapter ('My Health Since the Blast') and accompanying footnote on page 209.

they sent a wave of heat through my internal organs setting off spasms once more. I wanted to shout at them to stop but could emit no sound. I felt them insert intravenous drips into the veins in my arm and ankle and attach electrodes to my chest to monitor my heart.

"Her blood pressure's gone under 50, she's not going to make it!" my doctor exclaimed. The head of department shone a light into my eyes and after examining them closely, shouted, "Don't give up yet, her pupils aren't fully dilated!"

I narrowly escaped death.

After the panic had settled, my doctor came to see me. Able to open my eyes again, I glared fiercely at him but I doubt my gaze was strong enough for him to notice. When he left, the doctor overseeing the patient in the bed next to mine came over. "You were very lucky that the Head was here on his routine round, and that we were all here at hand too," he said. "You wouldn't have survived otherwise." Apparently, they had planned to give a number of the other patients ACTH injections after me but in the light of my shock reaction, abandoned the idea.

"You saved our lives!" the patients exclaimed.

For days afterwards I was given blood transfusions. A large tunnel-like contraption was attached to my bed and I spent the next ten or so days resting quietly inside it.

Incidentally, the hospital assigned a carer, a quiet, middle-aged woman, to tend and watch over me. "Are you Christian?" she enquired with some reserve once I had recovered somewhat. "For some reason, whenever I'm beside you I feel calm and content." I can't say for certain but suspect it's because I accept my fate that she felt that way.

Some forty-five years after the atomic blast, I received a telephone call from a woman claiming to know me. She had firstly rung my mother to ask after me. Mother told me about the call but I had no recollection of the woman. "Remember, before the blast, she was living in the house diagonally opposite us?"

"I have no knowledge of any such woman."

"You don't? That's strange! Don't you remember, they were a large family with many children….," she prompted, adding when I didn't respond, "On the day of the blast, her older brother, who had recently arrived home from Yokohama, called out to me when I crawled out from under our collapsed house, and urged me to follow him."

"Ah, now that you mention it, I vaguely recall a man..." After this telephone conversation with mother, the woman rang me directly. From what she said, it appeared we had been close friends. But no matter how much she explained, I had no memory of her. Finally, in exasperation, she burst into tears at the other end of the telephone line.

"Fumi-chan, what on earth's gotten into you? It's me, Mitsuko. Pull yourself together, please!"

She persevered, explaining that after houses were torn down to create a fire buffer, we used to go together every day to collect scraps of leftover wood to use as firewood to heat the bath. "Remember, we went to......and then to...." As she talked, I felt some vague distant memories gradually begin to return; that there had indeed been someone like her, that we had indeed done those things and, what's more, that we had been as close as a pair of twins. Evidently, I had sent the occasional letter to her home in Yamaguchi Prefecture, where she and her family fled after the blast, describing Hiroshima's recovery. And then, when she married and visited Hiroshima with her husband, I'd met them at the station and guided them around the city on foot. But after that, I was in and out of hospital in Tokyo with that intractable illness, and in the struggle simply to survive, lost contact.

The year she phoned, I decided to make a detour through Yamaguchi Prefecture and visit her on my way back to Hiroshima for my grandmother's memorial service. As the train neared the station where she would be waiting, I grew increasingly anxious; I couldn't for the life of me remember what she looked like. The station was virtually deserted. I disembarked and stood on the platform with the uneasy feeling of a foreigner. Mitsuko rushed over, looking exactly like one of the women living in our neighborhood before the blast. That night, we stayed up all night chatting and gradually, one by one, her stories revived fond memories from the distant past.

It came as a big shock to me that I had lost those memories. My worst wound from the blast had been above my left ear. *Might I have suffered damage to that region of my brain? And were there other memories that I had lost, in addition to those to do with Mitsuko?* I decided to go to the hospital for some tests. The hospital gave me a CT scan and checked my memory, reflexes, reactions, and so forth but could find no abnormalities. "It's only natural after the shock of a catastrophic event like the atomic blast," the doctor had said, dismissing my concerns. But even now, I can't escape the feeling that somewhere in my brain is a gaping hole.

Another symptom of radiation poisoning is cataracts. In 1947, when I underwent a regular staff health check after joining the Communications Bureau, I was found to have cataracts. "Make sure you wear sunglasses whenever you go outside." At the doctor's strong advice, I bought some sunglasses but didn't use them; in those days only special people like movie stars wore sunglasses. I did find it strange that my eyesight, previously so good, had deteriorated so. My eyes would become extremely tired, making me feel stiff all over. Regardless, I felt lucky to be able to see when at the time of the blast I thought I'd gone blind, and in any case, I was consumed with trying to survive, there was no room in my life to think about making regular trips to the hospital simply to improve my eyesight.

I was sixty-three years old when I finally had the cataracts removed. First they operated on my right eye. After the operation, I was amazed at how good it felt to see things clearly. The pages of books were white, the letters black. But to my left eye, which hadn't yet been operated on, the color of the pages appeared beige, and the typeface, grey. A feeling of regret at the many months and years that I'd suffered from restricted eyesight, and anger over the dropping of the atomic bomb, resurfaced. For several months after the operation on both eyes, I enjoyed clear eyesight but it wasn't long before my eyesight began to deteriorate again. I was informed that my corneas had grown cloudy. After receiving laser treatment, burning around thirty holes in each eye, my eyesight recovered to roughly 20/25 vision. When I underwent tests later, however, it had dropped back considerably even with spectacles on.

When I was in my forties, I was told by an orthopedist that my bones were like those of someone in their mid-seventies or so. That makes sense for I've cracked my ribs a good ten times to date and in 2003, when I was travelling around the world promoting peace and the anti-nuclear message, I had a fall in Norway and was taken by ambulance to a local hospital where I stayed for approximately ten days, returning home in a wheelchair. It was found that I had smashed a vertebra in my upper spine and also cracked one in my lower lumbar. I was encased in plaster from my chest down to my buttocks and laid up in bed for four months. I've since recovered greatly but continue to receive nursing care once a week after being diagnosed by the doctor as meeting the government guidelines for moderate care.

Fortunately, on the day of the blast, father escaped serious injury. It was because he was fit and well that my immediate and extended family were reunited. He walked all over the city on August sixth in search of family, traversing it from east to west, then north to south, and did the same the following day, August seventh, this time in search of me. Then after that, he put his heart and soul into building our huts and creating a vegetable garden. I have no doubt that he suffered from the secondary effects of radiation exposure. For many years afterwards he was plagued with acute anemia and purpuric rashes – purple bruise-like rashes that would appear all over his body much as if someone had pressed their thumbs hard into his flesh. Several days later, the rashes would vanish only to be replaced by others. "This is a *pika* symptom," my father declared from very early on but there was no pain accompanying the rashes and he had neither the time nor money to seek medical attention. Mother and I also came out in purple rashes but they were nowhere near as bad as father's. Several years later, ABCC staff came to see father and had him hospitalized. I expect they realized the anemia and purpuric rashes were due to the effects of radiation. At 89 years of age, father slipped when getting out of the bath and died from a brain hemorrhage, but he'd apparently been showing symptoms for some time of advanced colon cancer.

Mother displayed various physical after-effects of radiation poisoning. Thirty-eight at the time of the blast, in her forties she required full dentures as a result of acute periodontitis.

Every day she would have several teeth pulled and return home looking as pale as a ghost. In those days, we had no money and suffered from chronic malnutrition. There weren't the effective medications that are available today and I doubt that they had good anesthetics. What's more, mother wasn't given any painkillers after the removal of her teeth. She found it too painful to eat or drink on days when her teeth were pulled and for several days afterwards could only take liquids. Regardless, there was no time for her to rest. She would have to head straight out to obtain food for us on the black market.

At that time people weren't free to buy food and yet we would have starved had we tried to survive on the paltry rations distributed by the city council. Indeed, there were daily reports then of people dying from starvation. So it was that almost everyone went out to obtain food directly from local farms, careful all the while to evade the watchful eye of the police. We had no money, instead we exchanged our best kimono and hanging scrolls, which had been sent to the countryside for safekeeping during the war, for a pitiful amount of rice and vegetables. This was called 'black marketing' because it was against the trading laws but it wasn't until later that a real black market sprang up in front of Hiroshima Station. A row of makeshift stalls selling goods acquired illegally from the Occupation Forces, goods of the Japanese Army, and no doubt stolen goods, this was a black market in the true sense of the word.[45] The local police officers would patrol the area but they

---

[45] In addition to goods such as rice and sweet potatoes diverted by farmers to the black market where they fetched far higher prices than on the legal market, a multitude of goods from military stockpiles, said to have been looted by militarists, industrialists, bureaucrats, and politicians in the post-surrender chaos, found their way onto the black market. According to Dower, a "frenzy of looting" occurred during the turbulent two weeks following the emperor's radio broadcast on August 15th 1945, in which he announced Japan's surrender, depleting some 70 percent of all army and navy stocks in Japan. A major portion of the remaining military stocks, valued at around 100 billion yen, subsequently "disappeared almost without a trace" after the occupation authorities turned them over to the government to be used for public welfare and the economic reconstruction. (Dower, *Embracing Defeat*, 112–4)

also had to buy on the black market in order to survive. Sadly, the black market flourished off the backs of the poor city folk.

Mother's problems with her teeth arose before the black market appeared. Her days consisted of searching for food, raising the children, doing the cooking and other such housework and, when she'd recovered enough strength after the previous removal, going to get more teeth removed. In this way, though still only young, she became a toothless granny, relegated to a soft food diet while she waited for her gums to heal. The day she came home with her full set of dentures, we looked at her and giggled, oblivious to her discomfort; two rows of large, white, artificial teeth filled her mouth, making her face appear long like a horse's, and when she laughed, she looked just like a horse whinnying.

After she got her false teeth, mother had a hysterectomy as a result of a growth that may have been malignant. Again, several years later, she developed stomach cancer and had both her duodenum and gallbladder removed along with a section of her stomach. Next, she developed diabetes. This was followed by heart disease – in her later years she had a pacemaker – then cataracts. The damage she suffered to her left arm at the time of the blast left it feeling numb but little by little over many months and years, the numbness faded naturally until it only affected her fingers. Cooking, laundry – there were no washing machines back then – and other housework required a lot of wringing by hand so mother felt greatly handicapped by her arm. To the day she died she continued to be afflicted by numbness in her left ring finger. Additionally, three shards of glass remained embedded in her upper arm. After her heart operation, she was diagnosed as being severely physically handicapped.

In her later years, mother developed many other physical problems. Of these, painful eyes and deterioration of her sight seemed to be the most trying to her. She virtually lost all sight in one eye, which had cerebral hemorrhaging, and both eyes developed many fine lines in the cornea, a phenomenon that even the optometrist found puzzling. An acute dry eye condition required eye drops every 30 minutes or so. Toward the end she was certified as suffering from moderate to severe dementia and in the evenings would disappear into her own world but during the day she was her usual self, giving everything and everyone her devoted attention.

Survivors of the atomic blast suffer from all manner of after-effects such as chronic anemia, cancer, osteoporosis, cataracts, not to mention leukemia, but one hears very little about abnormalities in the body's various orifices and mucous membranes. For over a decade, I suffered from festering lips, and my mother, aunt, older sister, and I all suffered from periodontitis. [46] Aunt Tomoko's ears constantly discharged bloody pus; she lost her hearing in one ear after the eardrum completely dissolved and is hard of hearing in the other. Goodness knows how many times she was operated on to remove tumors in her armpits. At the same time, one of her kidneys developed cancer and was removed, and she had two operations on her colon. Every time she was operated on, the wound took considerable time to heal. She is now in her nineties, has undergone nine major operations to date and, due to various fractures, relies on walking sticks in both hands to get around.

My sister suffers from periodontitis, bone fractures, peptic ulcers, migraines, and glaucoma. I list my own illnesses later. Like me following the blast, my younger brother suffered from frequent nose bleeds after he returned from the countryside to live with us in our hut. Our nosebleeds continued into adulthood and were a source of concern for our mother.

Another illness that survivors struggled with is an affliction called the atomic bomb *burabura-byō*; one appeared normal in all respects but felt constantly sapped of energy and profoundly lethargic. As a result, survivors struggled to find employment or a marriage partner. Indeed, some of the affected were deemed 'lazy' and either forced to relinquish their jobs, accept a divorce, or consciously made such choices themselves. I had left Hiroshima in order to get treatment for the intractable illness I'd been diagnosed with, said to affect the entire body, so it wasn't until some years later that I heard about the symptoms of the *burabura-byō* affliction. In my case, this

---

[46] A serious gum disease that damages the soft tissue and bone that surround and support the teeth. Untreated, it can lead to tooth loss and increase the risk of heart disease and other health problems.

illness affected me day and night for many decades. So exhausted did I feel, I would pray before bed not to wake next morning. There were times when I pleaded with the doctor; "Please, just for a day, or an hour even, can't you do something to dispel the heaviness in my limbs?" But the doctor refused explaining,

"It's a symptom of your illness (Erythematodes), it can't be cured." I believed him, thinking that it may also be due to physical and emotional exhaustion brought on by illnesses and the struggle to survive. The lethargy gradually faded once I reached my sixties and seventies, but I could never hope for a full recovery.

No doubt, each and every survivor has had to secretly live with all sorts of emotional and physical pain.

Incidentally, around thirty or so years ago, in Yokohama as I recall, physicians gathered from all over the world to hold a panel discussion where they reported on the results of their research and exchanged ideas on the effects of radiation on the human body.

According to those discussions, they had more or less clarified the damage caused by radiation but one area remained to be explored, and that was the study of residents in Hiroshima immediately after the bomb was dropped, living off food that was either growing or cultivated on the land there. Listening in the audience, I was sorely tempted to raise my hand thinking that I could perhaps assist. But suddenly from somewhere deep within arose a profound fury, silencing me. Deep in my heart, I still harbored a fierce anger toward the ABCC and the day it stripped us of our humanity.

# ABCC

"Poor souls," Mother would say whenever she witnessed natural disasters, wars, refugees, or famine on television. "Then again no one helped us at the time of the *pika* bomb," she would add after giving it some thought. "No one gave us any food, clothing, or anything at all, did they? We drank rainwater and received no treatment for our injuries. It's amazing how we survived!" Certainly, our injuries were left to heal naturally. This didn't strike us as strange in such extreme conditions where each and every day was a struggle simply to survive. Stretched to our emotional and physical limits, we had no inclination to seek assistance.

There are a number of things that I learned of years later. Immediately after the dropping of the atomic bombs, astounded at the unprecedented damage and atrocities they caused, the Japanese government registered a strong protest against America for 'having used inhumane weapons in contravention to international law' via the neutral state of Switzerland. Domestically, however, the government hid the truth, reporting only that a 'new type of bomb' had been dropped, and minimized the extent of the damage. They did this out of concern for the civil unrest and loss of morale the news might cause. As for America, the devastation and horrific suffering in the aftermath of the blasts went far beyond their imaginings. To avoid world criticism and ensure they could control all investigations into the physical destruction to the cities wrought by the bombs and the effects of radiation exposure on humans, they sealed off Hiroshima and Nagasaki to the international community and media. They are even said to have refused International Red Cross assistance. All Japanese medical activities and media reports were placed under the control of the American authorities, while survivors were forbidden from talking about the bombings even among themselves. In this way, Hiroshima and Nagasaki were closed off from the outer world and we were deliberately left to our own devices.

When the American occupying forces came to Hiroshima after the war, they constructed a building for their 'Atomic Bomb Casualty Commission', or ABCC, at the summit of Mt. Hiji which afforded a panoramic view of the city. The Commission immediately began surveying the various forms of damage caused by the atomic bomb. The sudden appearance of this silver building glittering on the summit seemed like an arrogant display of power by the victor, making us feel all the more wretched in our shacks thrown together from scraps of wood and corrugated iron salvaged from the charred wasteland to keep us dry at night. Presently a rumor spread that the building was a hospital and the expectation among survivors that we might receive some medical treatment grew.

Before long U.S. Army jeeps began to drive around the city picking up survivors and taking them to the ABCC. In my case, an American dressed in military uniform suddenly appeared before me and, directing me to get into his jeep, virtually took me there by force. At the ABCC, I was taken to a room already packed with people; young and old, male and female all crammed in together. Several American soldiers stood outside the entrance. We were all standing around in a daze, each clutching a sheet of cloth we'd been handed, when a soldier came in and instructed us through the use of body language to remove our clothing and pull the cloth sheet over our heads. Spreading out the cloth, I discovered that it had an opening in the center, a poncho in other words. We were reluctant to remove our clothes in a room full of people, especially in front of the opposite sex, but pressed on by the soldier felt obliged, in the end, to comply.

Averting our eyes from each other, we hastily changed. Everyone was clearly mortified.

Amid the anxiety and strain of wondering what would happen to us next – and possibly because I felt cold – I suddenly felt the urge to pee. Several people followed as I asked the way to the toilet, no doubt just as anxious as I was. We had to go down a corridor and turn at the end into another passageway that led outside. The toilet sat at the very end of the passageway. Several soldiers stood guarding the exit. Open space above and below the toilet doors meant that you were only hidden from view when crouching down. I could see the feet of those waiting next in line, making it difficult to settle and do my business.

Next we were led, in our ponchos, to a large room for tests. I don't recall much apart from having my wounds examined and blood tests taken but I can still clearly visualize the beds and various medical apparatuses that I threaded my way through, receiving tests along the way, before finally exiting the room. It was a deeply humiliating experience, with none of the human contact that would normally exist between a doctor and his or her patient; we were simply treated like objects.

Today, survivors who undergo tests at the ABCC are apparently referred to as 'collaborators' and treated like human beings but in those days the tests were compulsory and I heard stories of young men remonstrating and young women breaking down into tears over going there because they would be made to strip right down, underwear and all, and then be photographed naked from multiple angles. The ABCC must have been investigating abnormalities in the development of the sexual organs, breasts, and pubic hair.

"The ABCC only conducts tests and doesn't provide any treatment," people began to complain and make excuses for not going. In reality, it was such a struggle for us to simply subsist, we had neither the time nor energy to expend on other things. After a time, rumors began to spread: "Lately, the ABCC will let you know if they discover any signs of illness and advise you to see a Japanese doctor." "I hear that if you allow them to do an autopsy when you die, they'll give you a magnificent funeral by way of thanks." One day, a neighbor passed away. One of those attending the funeral saw the coffin quietly removed from the funeral wagon and placed into an ABCC car waiting at the crematorium. After removing the internal organs, the ABCC returned the body to the crematorium where the family came to collect it the following day. The family said that they were shown no gratitude, let alone provided with a funeral service.

The survivors became increasingly uncooperative, obliging the ABCC to gradually change its approach. They began giving food to starving children, and gifting towels, thermometers, and the like to adults. Survivors would be transported by taxi and even served refreshments at the institute while awaiting the taxi home. Eventually taxis were given permission to drop the survivors off wherever they wished on the trip back, and certificates of gratitude were given to those who willingly cooperated – my mother received a few of these, and when, several years back, one of the women in our old neighborhood passed away, they apparently found several such certificates in her belongings. When undergoing tests, each survivor would be assigned a Japanese staff member, and provided with an individual changing room fitted with a locker. Some would be administered medicine, others given tests for admission into hospital. My father was one of the latter – as mentioned earlier, father didn't receive any injuries as such at the time of the blast but was plagued with anemia and purpuric rashes afterwards. Father said he was treated very well by the ABCC while in hospital.

Only those whom the ABCC determined had radiation poison-related diseases were administered medicines or admitted to hospital – I expect providing medication was all part of the institute's research. Regardless of the degree of radiation poisoning, almost everyone was sick and wounded or physically and emotionally weak and emaciated after the blast; few were in good health. The lives of many were compromised as a result of serious wounds, starvation, or shock but the ABCC appeared to show no interest in these people. Aunt Hatsuyo suffered from heart disease for many years. Her husband, Uncle Shūzō, developed cancer and thereafter received regular check-ups at the ABCC. My aunt also sought a check-up but was refused. One morning, she had a heart attack while doing the laundry. She was discovered, dead, with her head submerged in the tub of water. When, a year later, my uncle died, the ABCC were round in a flash, asking permission to conduct an autopsy on his body. The family rejected their request.

I was only a child when the jeep turned up and took me in to the ABCC for tests. Nevertheless, from that time onwards, I harbored a vague sense of distrust and dislike of the United States of America – not the American people but the United

States as a powerful nation. I believe that the atomic bombings of Hiroshima and Nagasaki were conducted by the United States out of their ambition for supremacy in the post-war world, and also as a human experiment.

It was my misfortune to fall victim to the atomic bomb. Nevertheless, if I could genuinely contribute to humanity in the post-Hiroshima-Nagasaki nuclear age, I would never refuse to do so. But to the researchers – which may well be normal from their perspective – we are simply research objects, human 'specimens' and 'cohorts' for their constant observation. The wrath that I have felt toward the ABCC ever since that day I was taken away by them for tests stems from a feeling of anger and indignation at their trampling on our humanity – we too were human, just like them!

1995 marked fifty years since the dropping of the atomic bomb. That year, and the previous year, my family held special memorial services. After the service one day, I made up my mind to visit the ABCC. On the day of my visit, it had been wet and cold all morning. It was many years since I last visited the summit of Mt. Hiji. A modern-looking art museum, library, park, and car park had been built up there although, perhaps because of the rain, there was no sign of any people. When the semi-cylindrical ABCC building came into view, I felt a sharp pain in my chest. The formerly shiny silver building had stagnated over the fifty years and signs of rust here and there sent a shiver through me.

The front entrance was locked. After knocking on the door and capturing her attention through the glass pane, a young female employee unlocked the door and ushered me in. Once she realized I had undergone tests there before, she became warm and friendly like we were old acquaintances. "As it happens, we're doing tests today so a number of people have come in. You may know some of them," she said, showing me the list of patients visiting that day. I couldn't see anyone that I knew on the list. Picking up the phone, she announced my arrival whereupon another staff member appeared, queried the purpose of my visit and, after encouraging me to provide my name and address, proceeded to give a general overview of the institute.

The ABCC is now the jointly run Japan-American Foundation for Research on the Effects of Radiation, [47] normally referred to as the 'Radiation Effects Research Foundation'. [48] The director is Japanese, the deputy-director American, while the staff comprises both Americans and Japanese. The branches of research include Clinical Studies, Pathology and Epidemiology, Genetics, Radiobiology, and Statistics. These are then divided into a variety of research divisions studying life expectancy, the effects of internal radiation exposure, cytogenetics, molecular science, cancer, cardiovascular diseases, and so forth. I was told that the departments' research results are loaded into the computer and the Foundation's vast quantity of data forms an important source of information for various international institutions.

My guide referred to me as a 'collaborator' and showed me round with an air of intimacy. In the corridor outside each of the research rooms and laboratories were noticeboards posted with explanations in English and Japanese, and various charts and diagrams, suggesting that the institute has many domestic and international visitors. The library contained rafts of reference works, giving a strong sense of the global importance of the Institute. But there was one matter about which I was not satisfied. Around thirty years ago as I recall, I refused to undergo follow-up tests at the ABCC. My written response to their request was as follows:

"Nuclear weapons, and additionally nuclear power plants, have proliferated, propelling the world into a nuclear age. The effects of radiation on the human body will continue to be a problem into the future. Unfortunately, I was made a victim of the atomic bomb. If my body and diseases could be of some assistance to humanity, I would be happy to cooperate. But I do not wish to be used as a guinea pig by the American and Japanese governments."

I subsequently received a very polite letter from the Director, Mr. Shigematsu Itsuzō, in which he repeated their request. Mr. Shigematsu wrote of various matters including the fact that the Foundation is a joint American and Japanese

---

[47] 放射線影響研究所
[48] 放影所

institute, that it makes global contributions, such as at the time of the Chernobyl disaster, and how he himself is a survivor of the atomic bomb. Moved by his revelation that he too was 'a victim of the atomic bomb', I relented and agreed to undergo tests.

Sometime after that, however, I had the opportunity to spend time with a group of children from Chernobyl when they visited Japan. My interest aroused, I subsequently read a number of books on the Chernobyl disaster. According to those books, the damage caused by the disaster was greater than it would otherwise have been due to the fact that, of all the international investigatory teams invited to visit the site, the Soviet government put their greatest trust in the opinions of the Japanese researchers who advised them that 'the levels of radiation are not such as would warrant concern.' I've also heard that among the Japanese who collaborated with the ABCC, are physicians from the former Imperial Japanese Army's biological and chemical warfare research and development unit, Unit 731,[49] made known to the public by the book *The Devil's Gluttony*.[50]

---

[49] Unit 731(731 部隊) was a covert unit of the Imperial Japanese Army that undertook human experimentation on men, women and children, the majority of whom were Chinese, during the second Sino-Japanese War (1937–45), WWII. The unit was based in Harbin, Manchuria, where Japan had established a puppet state. Researchers involved in Unit 731 were never tried for war crimes at the end of the war, as the American government gave them immunity in exchange for data obtained in the experiments, and the Japanese government has never officially acknowledged the unit's atrocities.

[50] *The Devil's Gluttony* (悪魔の飽食, Vols. 1 & 2, Kōbunsha: 1981–1982) by Morimura Seiichi exposed the atrocities committed by Unit 731. The work became a best seller in the early eighties but was temporarily withdrawn from the market when it was discovered that Morimura had at times confused Unit 731's operations with Unit 100, another Imperial Japanese Army facility developing biological weapons during World War II, and falsely attributed unrelated photos to Unit 731. In 1983, a revised edition appeared under Kadokawa Publishing House (cf. http://en.wikipedia.org/wiki/Unit_731). For more information, see

According to the Foundation's research results to date, *hibakusha*, or survivors of the bombings, suffer from various effects of radiation but they say they can find no abnormalities in second-generation *hibakusha*.[51] They are now at the stage of investigating third generation *hibakusha*, but apparently can't find any collaborators. As a collaborator, I gained special entry into the administration office where they showed me my mother's and my medical files. According to our files, my mother was being studied under the Life-span study program while I was part of a document survey – as an aside, thirty-five percent of the twenty thousand people being studied under the life-span program had passed away by then.

Sitting out on the desk was the file of a friend of mine who, as a child, was among those being studied under the growth and development study program. There was a note on the file indicating that her records had been sent to a certain research laboratory. My friend moved to Tokyo over forty years ago, married and settled in Chiba where she has lived ever since. She loathes the ABCC and is adamant she has never responded to any of their requests for follow-up examinations since leaving Hiroshima. Regardless, to this day, her file is still active. It's been over fifty years since I left Hiroshima, and for my friend, a good forty years, and yet it would appear that the

---

Nozaki, Yoshiko, *Textbook controversy and the production of public truth: Japanese education, nationalism, and Saburo Ienaga's court challenges* (University of Wisconsin: Madison, 2000).

[51] The dearth of evidence of abnormalities among second (and third) generation *hibakusha* can, as some scholars have pointed out, be put down to a lack of documentation and reporting of miscarriages, bearing of deformed children and other such experiences of women *hibakusha*. This would appear to stem, on the one hand, from a lack of questioning by researchers and, on the other hand, a reticence on the part of women *hibakusha* to discuss such matters for fear of discrimination against themselves and their offspring. For a discussion of these issues see, for example, Kate Dewes, 'Women *Hibakusha* from Hiroshima and Nagasaki Talk about Genetic Effects' (in Busby, Chris. *Wolves of Water*, 260–63).

Radiation Effects Research Foundation continues to keep records on us and include us in some study or other.

As I walked along the building's dingy old corridors and across its rain-swept connecting passageways, my heart grew cold and heavy. The doors to the former mortuary and autopsy rooms were tightly closed. "Family of the bereaved throw salt[52] and spit at us. Not that I don't appreciate their feelings," said my young guide. But I doubt that she will ever truly understand how we feel.

When the Foundation was still the ABCC, it conducted between three to four thousand autopsies a year but these were discontinued once willing collaborators fell to twenty percent, down from fifty percent in the early days after the bombing. Around the time of my visit, a documentary on the religious cult *Aum Shinrikyō* ('Aum Supreme Truth')[53] had been televised; titled 'Satyam',[54] the program had taken up much of the day. As I made my way around the complex of research rooms, computer and x-ray laboratories, resource rooms, equipment laboratories, and administrative offices containing facilities for printing the foundation's publications and other resource materials, I was reminded of the documentary on the cult and an unbearable feeling came over me. Once I'd finished looking around, the young guide ordered me a taxi. I waited for the taxi in a dimly lit conference room. Needless to say, I had to pay for the fare.

I trudged around the deserted Peace Park. A suffocating sense of powerlessness and anger welled up inside me. I felt estranged. We were made victims of the atomic bomb. Now there are people exploiting the victims to investigate the effects of radiation on the human body. And there are people who believe that the dropping of the atomic bombs brought the war to an end. Then there are those who claim that nuclear

---

[52] Salt has been used from ancient times in Japan to cleanse oneself when one believes they have been 'polluted', and to ward off evil.

[53] Founded in 1984 by Asahara Shōkō, the cult gained international notoriety in 1995 when it used the nerve agent sarin to carry out a chemical attack on the Tokyo subway system. Twelve people were killed and a further 6,000 required medical attention. Trials of the cult leaders are still ongoing.

[54] Sanskrit for 'truth'.

deterrence has saved the post-war world. Or those who seek refuge under the nuclear umbrellas of the militarily powerful nations…what folly!

But then what could I do? I felt strangely empty and miserable at the sight of the Hiroshima Peace Memorial Museum's angular buildings which looked cold and bleak enveloped in rain. *What does it mean to be human? What is it that we seek and for what purpose do we live?* I wondered. I walked across to the Atomic Bomb Memorial Mound and the other monuments erected in memory of those who died. Only then, before the many voiceless souls of the dead, did I finally find some peace of mind. Memories of the day of the blast and the many days of my life since then quietly returned. Time stopped and in the chilly spring rain I felt myself gradually merging into one with the people resting there.

(Postscript 1) Some days later, when I looked over the Radiation Effects Research Foundation pamphlet, I found that, just as I suspected, we were described as 'specimens', and 'human cohorts'. These are no doubt suitable expressions from their point of view but I struggle with the thought of those physicians engaging excitedly in conducting autopsies and studies, and making records of the rare 'objects for experiment' that appeared all of a sudden in enormous quantities after the blast. No doubt there were those among them who, as fellow humans, wrestled with their consciences. I hear that some of the American physicians returned home after becoming disillusioned with a role that dictated that 'physicians must not provide medical treatment', or departed with the words, 'next time I'll come on my own.' Others apparently became anti-nuclear, peace activists after witnessing the tragic aftermath of the atomic bomb. *Were there any such people among the Japanese physicians?* Sadly, I have heard of none to date. Another point I'd like to emphasize is that the ABCC's inhumane studies and follow-up surveys were being conducted after the end of the war; indeed, they are still being conducted today, although they may fall under a different name.

For those at home in Japan or abroad who think, 'The atomic bombing happened during wartime and it's no different from other cities that suffered attacks,' I'd ask them to consider why it is that the United States went ahead and dropped the

116

atomic bombs when they knew it was just a matter of time before Japan surrendered.

After my visit, I was sent another follow-up survey from the Radiation Effects Research Foundation, a 'Health and Lifestyle Survey', marked 'private and confidential'. 'The information you have provided is precious. We humbly request your cooperation to help us further advance the Foundation's research activities,' said the accompanying letter. I never submitted the form. Neither did I respond to a survey sent out by the Ministry of Health and Welfare, although I may have returned it with comments.

(Postscript 2) In July 2012, NHK broadcast a special documentary on internal radiation exposure during which they touched on the ABCC. Prior to that, the ABCC had never been reported on and, until recently, few people knew about the Foundation even in Japan. Extensive coverage was given to a man who had been a toddler riding on his mother's back at the time of the blast and about how, upon request, he had acquired a copy of his medical record from the ABCC. According to the documentary, many survivors now have copies of their records.

In July 2005, I returned to Hiroshima to hear the NHK Hiroshima Children's Choir give a performance of my poem, *Prayer for Water*, set to music by composer Wakamatsu Masashi[55] at a concert commemorating sixty years since the dropping of the atomic bombs. While there, I met up with a close childhood friend, Nishioka Seigo, and at his encouragement, sought copies of my parents' and my medical records from the ABCC. We were told at the time that Nishioka was only the second, and I the third person to request copies. My record was written in English with a short blurb attached in Japanese. The moment I read it, I intuited that it was fake. The notes stated that I suffered from ill health and my mother had brought me to the ABCC many times. Dates and times of visits, blood test details and medical examination results were all recorded. Anyone seeing the file would take it for the truth but as outlined earlier, I had a strong aversion to the ABCC and have no recollection of making frequent visits.

---

[55] 若松正司 (1928–2009)

There was the one occasion when I went on my own, out of desperation, seeking advice on the possible causes of, and treatment for, the dreadful disease afflicting my lips. The results of an examination proved inconclusive but I was told there was one possible cause; gold jewelry! Apparently, in the past, a member of the British royal family had suffered from symptoms similar to mine. After various tests, it was discovered that the woman had an allergy to the gold jewelry she wore. The administrator at the ABCC took me to their large library where she pulled out a book on the royal family and, pointing to a section in the book, said, "Look, it's described here." The lives of survivors of the atomic bomb were not such that we could adorn ourselves with gold jewelry and the like.

Nishioka likewise considered the records to be fabricated. "Attached to the copy of my record is a thank you letter they claim I wrote to the ABCC but there's no way that a thirteen or fourteen-year-old could have penned a letter like that," he said. "And for starters, I have no recollection whatsoever of writing it."

Various other aspects of the NHK documentary, in addition to its coverage of the ABCC, differed from my memories of my actual experiences. *So this is how history is created and passed on to future generations,* I thought despondently after viewing it.

# Hesaka Primary School

Aunt Tomiko, my older sister, and I finally arrived at Hesaka Primary School on the evening of August seventh. The school grounds were strewn with bodies of the dead and dying. We picked our way through the small gaps between them, obliged at times to stretch out a leg and step right over them. We were put up for the night at a farmhouse adjacent to the school grounds that belonged to a distant relative of father's. Initially we were able to make a bed for ourselves on top of straw in the barn but it wasn't long before we were driven out into the garden by the steady arrival of other evacuees, especially members of the army who expected to be given priority. My brother's body was likewise moved from under the veranda to a bare patch of earth in the garden.

That night, smoke rose all night long from a funeral pyre in the grounds of Hesaka Primary School after those who were still alive and mobile proposed to pile all the bodies up in the center of the school grounds and cremate them. It was a painful ordeal. A massive mound of some three or four hundred bodies was made and still the bodies kept coming. "They won't burn if we stack them up any further." Many times a fire was lit, only to fizzle and die almost immediately. "Maybe we should pour some more oil over?" "No, I'd say there's not enough firewood." "Let's light it from all sides?" "Hang on, please don't add any more bodies. We can burn them with the next pile."

After copious amounts of kerosene were poured over the mountain of bodies, the fire finally caught hold. But then the bodies began to wave about among the flames as if they were still alive. "Hey, they're alive!" a mother shrieked and calling out her child's name, tried to leap into the flames. The mother was dragged away from the flames and pinned down by a

119

middle-aged man. "Let me go, my child's alive! Give me back my child!" she screamed frantically as she tried to race back into the fire.

"It's hard, I know, but control yourself please! My wife's in those flames too!" The man restraining the screaming woman released her and wept.

Had the Murai's son, Hiroshi, seen any family before he died? I slowly circled the perimeter of the enormous fire. Human beings heaped high and burning like a pile of black logs. Until yesterday morning, most of these people were ordinary civilians living quiet, uneventful lives. How could they have been reduced to this tragic state in just one day? People with whom we'd exchanged friendly conversation no longer individuals but part of a burning mass of anonymous corpses. Young and old unceremoniously incinerated, with no one to watch over them or give them a Buddhist service, and deaf to words of parting from family members. My face grew hot in the heat from the kerosene-fueled blaze of burning bodies. I felt as if I were burning up with them. Large flames stretched high into the sky, and above the flames, climbing even higher into the heavens, was a trail of deep crimson smoke.

Later, we lay down our exhausted, wounded bodies on the cold earth in the garden of the farmhouse. Like the school grounds, it was packed with the wounded. All night long, the stars twinkled in the sky, a sky filled with the stench of burning bodies. Below the stars floated a wispy layer of white cloud, so close I felt I could almost touch it if I stretched out my arm. As one cloud drifted away, another would appear then gradually sail off. Earlier in the evening, the heavens had been a hot, raging, golden inferno, now there was a cold, clear, starry sky. "Hideo-chan, Hideo-chan." My mother kept calling my brother's name as if delirious. Her sad, mournful tone sent a shiver through my veins. Never had I heard my mother, who always had such a sunny disposition, sound so heartbroken. *If only I'd died instead of my brother*, I thought regretfully time and again as I listened to her grieving.

I passed a sleepless night that night as I gazed up at the clear sky glittering with the many stars that formed from the steady stream of lives rising up to the heavens.

# End of the War

The Murais and their extended family drove four posts into the rubble, threw some charred corrugated iron over top, and knocked together a shack on the burned-out ruins to keep the dew off them at night. Aunt Tomiko, my older sister, and I spent several days there in their care; thirteen of us huddled under the one roof in a space of no more than two tatami mats, or just under 3.5 square meters in area, to keep dry. Mr. Murai's wife, her leg injured and hideously swollen, sat up all day and night, leaning against one of the posts for support. With no room for us to lie on our backs or fronts, regardless of burns and abrasions, we slept on our sides, closely huddled together, those in the middle bending their legs as much as possible, those on the very outside just managing to keep their heads under the corrugated iron. No one had the energy to flatten the rubble underneath the shack; it bit into our flesh at night but out of consideration for each other, no one moved. Room didn't allow for turning over in the night.

In the daytime, we sweltered in the blazing heat of the sun which beat down relentlessly on the scorched earth, while throughout the night until dawn, it felt as cold as winter on the scorched plains – or perhaps our physically weakened state meant we felt the cold and heat more keenly? It was so dark at night on the ruins it was almost as if we'd been wiped off the face of the earth. In that bottomless blackness, we received bodily warmth, confirmation that we were alive, and, I think, tacit encouragement from each other. What did we eat to survive? And how did we pass time during the day? We saw no other people, no animals of course, in that world of ours. I think we spent our days in a severe state of shock, waiting, in the scorching heat of the day, for the cool after sunset, and longing, in the cold, jet-black night, for the bright, warm sun. No rescue team or relief supplies reached our district.

On August 15th, I was wandering vacantly along the street behind Hakushima Primary School. My brothers and sisters had all studied at Hakushima Primary, and it was in these school grounds that my younger brother, who died from the atomic blast, had been showered with the bomb's scorching rays of light. On summer evenings, before the bomb, they used to hold a fair once a week along this street, a relatively broad lane on the school's northern boundary that we called 'the back road'. The street would be lined with all manner of stalls; sweet stalls, toy stalls, stalls where you could try to scoop goldfish out of a tub with a paper spoon. I remember walking around the dimly lit street, the air thick with the smell of acetylene gas, hanging off Uncle Torao's arm (the one who died from the blast) with my cousin with whom I was very close.

The day after the bomb was dropped on Hiroshima, my mother, older sister, and I had stood in a daze for some time among the ruins of our house before returning to Nakagawara along the 'back road' behind the school. Just as we turned into the street, a strange sight caught my eye: in the northern back corner of the school grounds were three small piles in a row, each containing the bones of what must have been a dozen or so bodies. After all the children from third grade upwards were evacuated to the countryside, Hakushima Primary served as a temporary lodge for soldiers passing through Hiroshima – Hiroshima was an army base and soldiers being dispatched to the battle fields would board freight ships at Hiroshima's Ujina Port. None of the soldiers were young. They would sit under the trees or in the shade of the school buildings to escape the burning sun as they ate their 'Japanese-flag' lunches of brown rice studded with a large red pickled plum. Whenever we were playing in the grounds, one or other of the soldiers would call out to us. "Hey, like to try some?" they would say. Or, "You know, I've got children at home about the same age as you." They wore forlorn smiles. We children were permanently hungry, most days a meager serving of potato and soy lees were all we had to eat. Rice was a rarity. Even so, we never accepted any food from the soldiers. If I recall correctly, the soldiers were at the school on the sixth of August. But why hadn't they escaped the blast? What had happened that they'd ended up stacked one upon the other, and incinerated?

I don't recall whether the piles of white bones were still there the day of August 15th when I was wandering absent-mindedly along the street behind the school. I was watching ominously large storm clouds gathering in the distance above Mt. Futaba which looked as if they would bear down on me at any moment. Suddenly, out of the clouds fell a shower of glittering objects. *What on earth...? Was I losing consciousness again?* Just as I was wondering, a plane emerged from the clouds and flew toward me, scattering the bright, glittering objects on its way. The plane passed overhead and continued on its course. The bright shiny objects were leaflets. I picked up one that fluttered down beside me. It was a notice announcing the war's end. I felt no emotion whatsoever at the words, 'end of the war'. So extreme was my condition, I was oblivious to pain despite serious injuries, felt no hunger despite no food, and had no real sense even of being alive. After a quick scan of its contents, I discarded the leaflet and staggered on aimlessly. That night, not a single member of our small group living together and supporting each other on the burned-out plains mentioned the leaflets.

After staying at the Murai's shack for several days, we moved to one that the Kagawa family had built. They were the second family, after the Murais, to build one. Their shack was likewise just a sheet of charred corrugated iron atop four posts, but it was bigger and what's more, they had a heap of straw that they'd picked up somewhere. At night, there'd be a lot of rustling as we burrowed into the straw and went to sleep. *What bliss!* Cocooned in the soft, warm, fragrant hay, and free to stretch my limbs and turn over in my sleep, I had my first good night's sleep in what seemed like an age. The shack stood alongside Sanyo Railway's main trunk line. I was sleeping blissfully when I was woken abruptly by the loud roar of a train, so close it felt as if it was about to pass right over me. I leaped to my feet and watched as a steam train passed along the tracks on the embankment, light spilling from its windows. *Light spilling from a train's windows? Ah, of course, no more blackouts, it was the end of the war!* It finally sank in that the war was over, a realization that was perhaps also a sign, though

ever so faint, of the life-force slowly reawakening in me as I lay
sound asleep in my burrow of hay.

# Living Beneath the Heavens

The stars in the heavens sprinkled light over the blackened ruins of the city, where not a single lamp shone.

Struggling to survive among the rubble, we virtually sizzled in the withering heat of the day, while at sunset it would suddenly turn chilly. One night, we hit upon the idea of heating the rainwater in the *goemon-buro* that had survived the fires, and taking a bath by turns. There were no buildings other than our tiny shacks, nor any trees; the city of death stretched out under the starlight as far as the eye could see. No one could see me and yet, young and female, I hid behind the bathtub to get undressed. I vaguely recall having changed from the underwear and trousers I'd been wearing at the time of the blast into some other clothes when we temporarily evacuated to Saka.

I was covered in cuts from shattered glass and several shards were embedded in my skin. Even so, except for the deep gash to my head, I was unconcerned. It's hard to believe now but at the time anything less than serious and life-threatening didn't rate as an injury, and we felt little pain. Later we marveled at how we had managed on the day of the blast to flee over the crumbled buildings in bare feet without incurring any injuries. Surely all that can account for this is that we were in an extremely heightened state of nervous tension or a physical and emotional state that cannot be explained by modern reason.

How many days had passed since I last bathed? I quietly slid into the warm water, and felt my body and mind gradually relax. A warm feeling of happiness spread through me. The surrounding dark burned fields melted into the night sky while a cold evening wind moaned as it swept through the star-studded heavens. I stretched my arms up high toward the sky, whereupon the stars at my fingertips slipped down my wet arms into the water, filling the bath with sparkles as they bounced upon the water's surface.

Half a month or so after the blast, grandmother's and my family constructed our A-frame huts, side by side. The Murais joined us, building a shack nearby that was properly enclosed this time with boards on all sides – three families cleaving together for survival on the burned-out ruins of Hiroshima. During the day, we wandered over the blackened earth in the blazing sun, dragging home the few surviving sweet potatoes from the army's charred vegetable plots, while at night, we burned scraps of wood gathered from the charred plains, and in the light and warmth of the fire, peeled potatoes for the next day's meal. For a period of time, this was our daily routine. It was also a wonderfully happy time for us; the kindling burned well, there were no attacks from enemy planes, and no restrictions whatsoever. While it was true that we were all hungry and injured, and next day any number of us might be gone, not one of us felt anxious. Free from cares, we spent our evenings roaring with laughter, like children.

Mr. Murai and my grandfather were at the center of all this revelry. It didn't matter whether their tales of the past or of daily trivia were ones of struggle and hardship, as soon as they joined the conversation, they would whip up a storm of laughter. We had no power, no money, no occupation or social standing, no desires even. Instead, we had this happiness, a wonderfully pure and simple elation at being alive at that moment, together.

When was it that things began to change? We were barely subsisting, living one day at a time, when into our lives came farmers from the outlying areas with horses and carts, collecting anything of worth, including the *goemon-buro*, from the ruins, and taking them away. People began to return to Hiroshima, erecting their own shacks, or coming in search of close family and relatives. Signs of human life now lingered in the city that had been reduced to ashes and little by little ordinary life returned. Those nights of bathing in the light of the stars, or laughing and chatting as we huddled in a circle around the bonfire gradually disappeared.

One day, without warning, Mr. Murai committed suicide. He left no suicide note, and no one knew his motives for taking his own life, all we knew was that he'd used cyanide. He left behind a wife with a serious thigh injury, and three little girls, two of primary school age, the third, only an infant.

# Sunset and the Crows

Even today, whenever I see a fearsomely beautiful sunset, I am reminded of the sunsets in Hiroshima after the dropping of the atomic bomb. Living then in a foggy daze, somewhere in limbo between life and death, I found sunsets so moving, they would make my chest constrict. Then, after sunset, would come the flock of black crows.

Fearsome sunsets, sinking over a desolate city of death!

As the insanely blue sky with its scorching midday sun began to turn cobalt blue, a coolish breeze would sweep down over the city. *Ah, another day over,* I would think. It's not that I regretted the passing of time, or harbored any hopes for the morrow. Nevertheless, sunset would find me standing alone in the burned-out fields gazing up at the sky as it turned from cobalt blue to soft lavender, then from soft lavender to deep lilac. Every evening, I would halt where I was and gaze up in rapture as the sky changed hue. Little by little, the skies darkened to a deeper shade of purple, then, just as the sun began to sink behind the gentle slopes of the hills in Koi district on the western side of the city, they would suddenly be awash with gold. The heavens shone brightly once more, dyeing the twilight sky a deeper and deeper gold. The skies, their brilliance restored, would send golden melodies coursing through my veins.

*Ah, I'm alive! How wonderful it is to be alive!* Each evening, I savored the fact that I was alive and able to witness the sunset. *If only I could write music…,* I would think as strains of music coursed through me. Though I knew nothing about music, these melodies, all similar in tune, would bubble up inside me, their beauty moving me to tears. Had providence looked benevolently on this fourteen-year-old girl who, though

128

close to death, still clung to her tender life, and each evening, momentarily revived feelings scarcely alive within her?

As dusk deepened and the sky darkened, I turned my eyes toward the north. The northern hills formed a dark silhouette against the dusky sky in which would appear a black spot, like a needle-prick. One black spot, then five, ten, one hundred; the spots rapidly proliferated and grew in size. Amid eerie cries, would come a huge flock of crows. Scattering as they alighted, the crows would spread their black wings, latch on to the corpses in the rubble, and begin pecking at the human flesh. With their wings open they looked large and ferocious. Glossy jet-black from their beaks right down to their claws, they gave out harsh, ominous caws. Such a gruesome, unearthly sight, it made me tremble in fear. The crows would take a corpse each and peck at it to their hearts' content until, all at once, as if responding to some kind of cue, they would head back in the direction of the northern skies.

Next morning, it would be father's job to cover with rubble the corpses in the area where the crows had alighted. One day, I saw him preparing to cremate one of the corpses.

When I approached, he stopped me saying, "Go away!" his tone unusually stern. The body turned out to be Junko's, a girl who had lived across the road from us – one year younger than me, Junko had been a real livewire tomboy. I could still recognize her features, despite facial burns, but she was badly disfigured from her chest downwards as a result of horrific burns. Her body was lying near to where our front door had been but I gather, from what mother said, that she was at home at the time of the blast so she must have crawled as far as our house before eventually getting caught in the fires. I watched as a thin trail of smoke from her burning body rose into the air, forming a light haze above the rubble, and kept a silent vigil until the smoke eventually vanished into the summer sky.

Junko's family, the Miyamotos, lived in a house across the way from ours, beyond several large fir trees. Residing in their house at the time of the blast were Junko, her mother, her older brother, who was unwell, her sister Sumiko, who was two or three years her senior, and upstairs, a single woman going by the surname of Harada (I don't think she was family). I had never seen Junko's father. I often chatted with Junko's sister

Sumiko but she was reserved and had a grown-up air about her, so it was with Junko that I played.

One April, some forty-five or six years after the dropping of the atomic bomb, when I returned to Hiroshima for my grandmother's memorial service, I visited an old friend, Matsui Mitsuko (née, Suenaga), living in Hōfu City, Yamaguchi Prefecture, and went with her to visit her mother in hospital. "She's pretty much gone senile, doesn't even recognize my name!" Mitsuko warned as she took me to the hospital but as soon as I mentioned how things were prior to the atomic bombing, her mother was immediately able to place me and began to talk about the blast, describing events in minute detail as if they only happened yesterday. According to her story of events, on August 6th, Mitsuko, her younger sister, and the younger of her two older brothers, had all left home early for work on the student labor scheme but the older brother was still at home. When the bomb was dropped, the two-story house collapsed and Mitsuko's mother was caught beneath it with her one-year-old, Tatsuko, wrapped protectively in her arms. Mitsuko's brother was the first to crawl out from the rubble. He was up on his feet and moving about when my mother clambered out from under our collapsed house, and it was he who called out to her to flee.

After much struggle, Mitsuko's mother was eventually pulled out alive from the wreckage of her home. She saw the woman residing upstairs at Junko's house standing there, injured and looking like a ghost with her hair flying out in all directions. "What on earth happened?" the woman was muttering in a daze. Between Mitsuko's and Junko's houses ran a small, narrow lane. A building had collapsed into the lane, burying Junko.

"*Niichan*, please help me! Please!" Junko implored of Mitsuko's brother.

"Wait a moment, Junko. I'll come and get you as soon as I've dug Tatsuko out." But it was proving extremely difficult to rescue Tatsuko. The fires came round. When Mitsuko's mother made to flee, he yelled, "I'll get Tatsuko out even if it kills me!" Meanwhile, Junko continued to cry for help. Tatsuko was half dead by the time she was pulled free – it was all they could do to escape with her.

"Every night, I hear Junko's cries," Mitsuko's mother confessed with a look of anguish.

Some time later, Mitsuko said to me, "Mother hadn't really gone senile. I'm certain of that now. She simply claimed she didn't know me because my visits weren't frequent enough. She was a shrewd woman, my mother!" Apparently, when she passed away at ninety-six, she said to Mitsuko at her bedside, "Goodbye, my dear Mitchan, and thank you."

Sumiko was the sole surviving member of Junko's family. After the atomic blast, she lived right next door to us, so close our two huts almost touched, in a tiny one-room hut with a small earthen-floored kitchen attached, built for her by an uncle who was a carpenter. Our hut was likewise only small with two *tatami* rooms and a wooden-floored kitchen-cum-dining room to house a family of five. My parents felt sorry for Sumiko and fussed over her just as if she were their own child. She had an arranged marriage, at nineteen or so, after which she bore three baby boys. Life was tough for everyone after the blast but it was especially hard for the young couple with three children born in quick succession. The husband began to drink and eventually disappeared. Sumiko had to leave her children in the care of an orphanage (there were many atomic bomb orphans) so she could go out to work but it was difficult to find a decent job and she ended up moving around with an itinerant construction gang. Sometimes, when the gang came to Hiroshima, she'd turn up at our place, putting on a brave face, but eventually she came no more.

Many years later, when my mother was still alive and well, two young men came to visit her in Hiroshima. They were Sumiko's grown-up children. Perhaps because their mother had been exposed to the effects of the bomb, the youngest boy had apparently been sickly and disabled (he wasn't able to walk or talk even as a two-year-old and used to crawl to get about) and had passed away at the orphanage. The pair raised by the orphanage had grown into fine young men. They said they'd managed to meet up with their father in Osaka and had come to Hiroshima in search of news of their mother.

Since then, I've heard no more news of Sumiko.

# Verdure

Father cleared away the rubble in front of our hut and planted some leaf-vegetable seeds. We were not hopeful they would sprout, it having been said that no plants or trees would grow in Hiroshima for the next seventy-five years. Within a matter of days, however, the surface of the soil was dotted with green. I could scarcely believe my eyes. Once sprouted, the seedlings grew at an astounding rate. After seeing nothing but fields scorched the color of burned umber, my heart leaped at the sight of the fresh verdure; here was pure life!

Vegetable seeds were not the only things to sprout; weeds broke through the rubble and grew robustly, spreading their greenery across the ground. Those of us living on the burned-out fields staved off starvation by picking and eating those weeds. One weed, called the 'railway weed', [56] grew particularly profusely – indeed, it became rampant, towering over us in no time. On one occasion a burglar broke into our hut, taking us by surprise; our life centered around eating and sleeping, it never occurred to us for a moment that burglars might be about or that we needed to lock our hut. Startled by our shouts on his detection, the burglar leaped outside and darted into a thicket of railway weed. We gave chase but soon lost sight of him in the dense thicket.

With the spread of weeds came a mosquito outbreak. Due, perhaps, to the effects of radiation, the mosquitos were large and vicious. Every day, when evening came around, we would gather together a pile of railroad weed and burn it as a repellent

---

[56] A type of mugwort called *himemukashi-moyogi*, originally from North America. From the Meiji era (1868–1912) onwards it became a common weed around railway lines and on barren land in the cities, hence the name.

but the weed gave off a thick foul smoke, enough to drive us humans, let alone the mosquitos, away.

Once life began to settle down, father dug a vegetable garden among the charred ruins. We were overjoyed when the strawberries he planted produced bundles of tiny bell-like fruit that then ripened. The sight of the fresh, juicy-red fruit injected life into my desolate heart. Mornings and evenings, I delighted in strolling through the strawberry patch. However, the strawberries spread profusely as if under a magic spell, until eventually father removed them completely and tried French beans and pumpkins instead. The French beans likewise produced an amazingly large crop. Initially, we delighted in the beans' refreshing aroma and subtle sweetness but in time, the mere sight of them was more than we could bear. The pumpkins were tasty with a light, dry texture, and filled the stomach; for a time, we virtually lived on pumpkin. They grew at a similarly abnormal rate; no fertilizer was applied and yet the plants produced loads of monstrously large pumpkins. Eventually, we tired of pumpkin. Surprised by the large crops that he could grow in the ruins, father dug a proper garden on the ruins of Hakushima Primary. Sweet potatoes, sesame, burdock, carrots, daikon, potatoes – they all flourished.

One day, father was tilling the vegetable garden when he yelled, "Hey, I've found some snake eggs!" We went to see. In the soil was a pile of what looked like hens' eggs. "They're *aodaishō* eggs," [57] spat father as he stomped off – he loathed snakes. It was the first time in my life that I'd seen snake eggs; glossy white, and slightly larger and longer than a hen's, their strange beauty sent an icy shiver through me. At the same time, I marveled at their amazing ability to survive the atomic blast.

The city council planted Himalayan firs and oleander throughout the city of ashes. I imagine one of the reasons they chose these plants is that they are fast growing. Even so, I expect they displayed a much faster rate of growth than originally anticipated. Transformed into a Himalayan fir forest back then, today, Hiroshima's Peace Park is a well-tended park of pines and flowering cherries. The rows of oleander shrubs,

---

[57] A Japanese rat snake. This is the largest snake in mainland Japan, growing to around 2 meters. It is non-venomous.

with their wild, fiery-red display, have likewise long disappeared. Meanwhile, Hiroshima is now a city of one million people, and looks just like any other burgeoning city in Japan, a fact that greatly saddens me.

I understand that at one point the oleander was considered a symbol of Hiroshima but survivors of the atomic blast, myself included, detest the fiery-red flowers of this shrub that grew so wildly in the scorched earth. That's because they are a potent reminder of the day of the blast. The flowering cherry is more soothing to everyone's soul. On the other hand, I prefer the natural-looking forest that used to grow in Peace Park to the orderly trees that grow there today.

# Bone Statue of Buddha

"Far in the distance, the ring of a bell; if we are to find the dead in this world, it will be in a form precisely of this kind." Out of respect for the feelings of the priest who intoned these words, I will refrain from disclosing the name of his temple.

After the blast, survivors created funeral pyres in the ruins of the priest's temple for cremating the bodies of friends and relatives who had died, thinking that at least they would be near Buddha. Gathering up scraps of wood from the scorched earth, and charcoal for lighting the pyre, they cremated their loved ones, though they themselves might not live to see the next day, such a wretched state – barely distinguishable from the dead – were they in. Torn apart with grief, crying until they could shed no more tears, survivors stood beneath the scorching sun and watched over the bereaved as they were slowly, and with difficulty, incinerated.

Once the bodies of the deceased, who not long before had been among the living, were reduced to flimsy white bones, surviving family members would gather some of the larger pieces of bone and take them away with them. As the days passed, thousands of people's bones were left to pile up in the temple grounds. The presiding priest gathered these up and with the help of a local mason, created a small statue of Buddha – a sad white statue less than thirty centimeters high – by crushing the bones and cementing them together with plaster. Every year, for ten days from the sixth of August through to *Obon*,[58] the statue would be enshrined in the main hall of the

---

[58] *Obon* designates a three-day period in the height of summer during which it is believed that the spirits of one's ancestors and deceased family members will return to visit the house altar. Special food offerings are placed at the family altar, graves are

temple. At times its face looked like that of Shakyamuni,[59] at other times it looked utterly human. Surviving relatives saw their loved ones in the statue and, as they stood before it, communed with the souls of the dead.

Family members of the deceased, and other survivors living in the vicinity of the temple, used to come to see the bone statue after attending the memorial at the Peace Park on August the sixth. Over time, they have grown old and no longer attend the memorial, choosing instead to gather at the foot of the bone statue of Buddha. If the survivors have seen the passage of time, so too has the bone statue, turning grey with dust accumulated over many decades. Each year, whenever the sixth of August came around, there would be fewer survivors, first three, then five fewer survivors and so on, gathered beneath the bone statue which likewise began to show cracks here and there in its dry frame. The presiding priest passed away. His successor continued to maintain the bone statue of Buddha. One day he remarked, "Really, we're not supposed to enshrine more than one Buddha but well…fifty years have passed since the bomb was dropped so I've decided to permanently enshrine the statue in a corner of the main hall. It's my calling I believe, to pray for the repose of those who died from the blast, having been granted life myself." "I could of course wipe off the dust," he added, "but the statue is so worn now and at some stage will fall apart completely. When it does, I hope to lay it to rest in our large communal grave – provided, that is, I can live that long." So it was that in his late seventies, he wanted, it seemed, to devote the remaining years of his life to the care of the bone statue of Buddha, a statue that would undoubtedly crumble in time.

---

visited and cleaned, and festivities are held to entertain the dead, including the well-known *bon-odori* dances. The timing of *Obon* differs according to region. In Hiroshima *Obon* falls around August 15th.

[59] Shakyamuni (or Sākyamuni), also known as Siddhārtha Guatama or Gautama Buddha, is the sage on whose teachings Buddhist ideology is based. He is believed to have lived and taught in north-eastern India some time between the sixth and fourth centuries BCE (cf. entry for 'Buddha', *Encyclopaedia Britannica*).

The statue's white bone body also contained the bones of my uncle who passed away on August 23rd, 1945, as a result of injuries from the blast. "May I ask a favor?" I said.

"What is it?"

"Would you mind if I took a photograph?"

"Go ahead." he acceded, "That'll be the bone Buddha's very first photo." After I returned home to Kamakura, I had the photograph of the statue printed; its face, I thought, resembled that of the presiding priest.

The priest passed away over a decade ago now. Gone too are the survivors who used to gather at the foot of the bone statue. Covered in cracks and dust, the statue lingers on in its corner of the temple.

# Children's World

After the blast, dangerous items were left lying around in the city, especially in the burned-out ruins of army-related facilities where army tanks, bayonets, and machine guns had been left abandoned, and cartridges littered the ground like fallen fruit.

My brother Mikio, a sixth grader at primary school (then called *kokumin gakkō*[60]) at the time, had returned to Hiroshima from the countryside where he'd been evacuated. Quick-witted, and full of curiosity, Mikio got up to no end of mischief. One day, when mother and grandmother were gathering charcoal from the scorched fields near the ruins of the Military Youth Academy, they heard a loud boom. "What on earth was that?" they said, straightening up.

"Amazing what dangerous tricks kids will get up to, isn't it? Only lucky they weren't injured!" muttered a man as he passed by. Not long before Mikio and his cousin, who was a year younger than Mikio and a regular playmate, had run off in the direction from which the sound of the explosion came. "Surely it's not..." my mother and grandmother were just exchanging anxious glances when the pair came racing back, their faces deathly pale. Mikio told them they'd found a type 38 rifle, a machine gun, and some live bullets strewn about in the old Academy grounds. "Let's try firing the rifle," he'd apparently suggested and, getting his cousin to stand guard, had

---

[60] Japan's *shōgakkō*, or 'elementary schools', were renamed *kokumin-gakkō*, or literally 'national people's schools' in 1941. The change in nomenclature reflected a dramatic re-visioning of education in war-time Japan with a shift in emphasis from, among other things, creating independent thinkers to one of raising citizens who would obediently follow the will of the emperor and State.

loaded the gun and pulled the trigger. A loud explosion tore through the air, the recoil giving my brother a jolt so violent he swore he'd smashed his shoulder blade.

Cartridges littered the ruins for what seemed like forever after the war, and children used to pick them up and play with them like acorns. There was an accident at Mikio's school one day where a child lost some fingers; several children had gathered around a desk and were playfully tapping a cartridge when it suddenly exploded, taking a few fingers with it. Even so, my brother continued to come home with his pockets stuffed full of cartridges which, at mother's scolding, he would reluctantly dump back at the ruins.

As I recall, it wasn't until the year following the atomic blast that we had an electric light installed in our hut, and even then, we'd had to firstly privately procure a pole before the electricity company would come and connect the power lines for us. Nevertheless, thanks to Mikio, my parents and grandparents had a small amount of kerosene for lighting a wick on those long cold nights after summer that year of the blast when the electricity hadn't yet been connected. Every day, Mikio would head out, returning with a full bottle of kerosene. Gradually, the hour of his return grew later and later. He never told a soul where he acquired the kerosene until one day, when I'd gone with him to the Academy to play, he said, "See that army tank?"

"Is it real?"

"Of course!" To be sure, there sat a large army tank. Up close, it looked black and formidable, and as strong as a fortress. While I was circling the tank, my brother jumped inside. He was in high spirits, peering out from the hatch and pretending to be a real soldier. After we'd been playing on the tank for a while, he said, "I'm going to gather some oil before going home. It's getting late so you can go on ahead if you like." Armed with a small stick and bottle he then disappeared into the tank where, deep in its bowels, there was an oil tank. Hanging upside down, he thrust his hand with the stick through the opening and stretched down as far as his armpit. Then, dipping his stick into the pool of oil at the very bottom of the deep oil tank, he began the painstaking task of transferring the oil, drop by drop, to the bottle. "When the tank was full," he explained, "it took no time to fill the bottle but not now that it's down to the last dregs…" The sun was already setting in the west when the oil in the bottle reached the three-quarter mark.

Little by little, people were building shacks and returning to our neighborhood to live. Several of the evacuated children returned. The main chore for children living on the burned-out plains was gathering charcoal and scraps of firewood but at every opportunity we would head down to the moat around Hiroshima Castle, alongside the Academy, which was a fun place for children to play. It also turned out to be an unexpected goldmine of lotuses to feast on. The inner moat, which lay diagonally across from the Academy grounds, would be smothered in lotuses. We would climb down to the moat from the Academy side, dexterously slotting our hands and feet into cavities in the moat's stonewall until we could reach the fruit. The younger children would be waiting above to take the fruit from us as we collected them. Afterwards, we would sit down on the ground and share the lotuses between us. Freshly picked lotuses are truly delicious. After removing the small rounds of fruit from the large, green, platter-like pod, we would peel back the light green skin to reveal the lustrous white flesh inside. How happy we felt when we bit into the flesh and our mouths filled with the fruit's soft sweet milk!

One pod of fruit was enough to reduce the pangs of hunger considerably. Several days on, however, all of the fruit at hand's reach had been picked. As we strained to stretch our hands and feet further down into the moat, we would take more and more risks. We had no idea how deep the moat was. There was the body of a dead horse in it, and for all we knew, there might be some human bodies submerged in there too. Undeterred, we stretched our arms and legs down further and further into the moat, resorting even to using a stick in an attempt to drag just one more pod of fruit closer. It was on one such occasion that a girl slipped and fell in. Within seconds, she'd sunk as far as her waist. When my brother swiftly dragged her out, she was covered in mud and hundreds of leeches. We stripped her down and carefully checked her body and clothing. It was difficult to remove the fat leeches latched on to her skin and blood squirted from the spots where we managed to pry them off. So it was that our harvest of lotuses gradually dwindled. Still we shared them around and felt happy.

The lotus leaves were also convenient as 'umbrellas' for adults and children alike, though the large leaves with their thick stems were a little on the heavy side for children. The rain would gather on the leaf umbrellas and form shiny silver beads, eventually merging into one large wavering silver moon that we would then send splashing to the ground. Rainy days would be fun playing such games and, sheltering under the large lotus leaves, we felt like dwarves in a fairy tale.

On another occasion, when I hadn't joined them, my brother, cousin, and several other children had gone to the moat to dig for lotus roots. Apparently, the entire group of boys and girls stripped down and clambered into the water. Goodness knows how they dug for the roots with their bare hands but it seems that they all managed to get some and were just heading home when they were stopped by some adults who were out in boats harvesting the roots – they were merchants who made a living from selling lotus root. At their shouts, the children scattered and fled when Mikio suddenly noticed that our cousin had been caught. A gentle, good-natured child, our cousin wasn't good at handling such situations. Fortunately, it turned out that the man who had caught him was a friend of grandfather. He not only let our cousin off, he also gave him some roots to take home for grandfather.

One evening we had sukiyaki for dinner. Normally sukiyaki meant a few green vegetables (or they may have been weeds) simmered in the fry pan but that particular night there were some small pieces of white flesh floating in the pan. "Mmm, this tastes good!" father exclaimed giving a broad smile at which Mikio looked exceedingly pleased with himself. Our suspicions aroused, mother, my younger sister, and I made no attempt to touch the meat. "Honestly, it's really tasty. It's valuable protein, you should eat it." At father's encouragement, I picked up a small morsel with my chopsticks and popped it in my mouth; it tasted like chicken. Several days later, I saw Mikio battling with something down by the tank that we used to collect rainwater for cooking. On closer inspection, I found that he had a large edible frog on the chopping board and was attempting to skin and chop it. The frog was vigorously trying to shake my brother's hold on its legs. Though clumsy with the knife, before long – indeed, in the blink of an eye – he'd skinned it. As I looked on, the skinless frog gave a hop. I screamed and fled inside.

"Mikio-chan, please, could you stop the killing. That may be the cause of my illness. Please don't do it anymore." So saying, my mother managed to convince him to stop bringing frogs home. But he told me later that he continued his daily hunt for frogs. In Tsuruhane Shrine, near Hiroshima Station, there were hundreds of frogs, and a man had begged him to catch some to feed his sick wife.

In September, one month after the blast, Hiroshima was hit by the Makurazaki Typhoon. [61] It took some time for the floodwaters to recede. Mikio built a raft from driftwood (he may have also used some scraps of charred corrugated iron) and had a great time on it with his cousin and friends. Additionally, the raft came in very handy for gathering firewood and taking the washing out to the clothesline. The clothesline was merely a couple of poles stuck in the ground with a narrow pole strung across them; the slightest puff of wind was enough to send the whole thing toppling into the muddy waters, washing and all. When it did, mother and grandmother would sigh, re-wash the clothing, and once more ask Mikio to take it out on his raft for drying. As the raft couldn't take the weight of the adults, it was my job to hang the washing out and bring it in. And so my brother would row

---

[61] Makurazaki Typhoon, or Typhoon Ida as it is known in English, struck Japan on 17 September 1945, landing in Makurazaki, Kyushu before travelling up to the main island of Honshu. Hiroshima Prefecture, which was still reeling from the atomic bombing only one month earlier, was hit hard by the typhoon; much of the city was flooded, twenty bridges were washed away, and approximately two thousand people died or were listed as missing, accounting for over half of the casualties nationwide. It is still the second largest typhoon on record in Japan. (see http://www.pcf.city.hiroshima.jp/virtual/VirtualMuseum_e/exhibit _e/exh1202_e/exh120209_e.ht ml; also
http://www.bousai.pref.hiroshima.jp/www/contents/131884942717 9/index.html)

around on his flimsy raft looking very pleased with himself while my mother looked on anxiously.

In Hiroshima Castle grounds, was a building belonging to the 'Daihonei', that is, the old military headquarters erected in the late nineteenth century at the time of the Sino-Japanese War.[62] The building was flattened in the wind created by the blast but survived the fires. We collected all sorts of items from there to make use of in our daily lives such as wood, bricks, and paper. "To think that I lugged home that gatepost with 'Daihonei Ruins' etched in it only for it to be damn well turned into firewood! What a waste, eh! It would have made a great memento, had we kept it," bemoaned my brother on a later occasion.

Beside the stone fence near the southern entrance to the castle ruins, was a monument with a poem commemorating Hara Tamiki engraved on it.[63] A survivor of the atomic blast, Hara Tamiki left behind countless atomic bomb poems as sad lamentations before ending his young life by throwing himself under a train. I wonder if the poem etched into the copper plaque on the monument at the ruins was written in his own hand – it was beautiful handwriting.

> *Engraved in stone of days long gone,*
> *Casting a shadow in the sands*
> *Amidst a crumbling world,*
> *The vision of a solitary flower.*

It pained me to see several marks on the plaque from what appeared to be thrown stones. Every time I visited, the monument would be more and more marked. *Who did this, and for what purpose?* I thought, the pain turning to anger. Then,

---

[62] 1894

[63] 原民喜 (1905–51). Hara was a novelist and poet, born and raised in Hiroshima. He moved to Tokyo in 1925 after being accepted into Keio University where he studied English literature but returned to Hiroshima in January 1945, to escape the fire bombings. Although he survived the atomic blast, his home was destroyed and his health badly affected. In 1946, he returned to Tokyo where he died in 1951.

one day, when we were walking past, my brother Mikio explained, "They're using it as a slingshot target."

After that, the monument disappeared. The area around the stone wall where the monument had stood seemed strangely empty, and my heart with it. Some years later, when I visited the spot again, I began to wonder whether there really had been a monument there. Might it have simply been a figment of my imagination, an illusion that I had conjured up?[64]

One day, I'd gone down to the river at low tide to collect some *shijimi* clams. "Tonight's *shijimi* soup," I said that evening as I poured the shellfish into a pot brimming with water and threw in some salt. My family drank the soup with great relish. After that, whenever I saw the tide was out, I would head down to the riverbank and gather shellfish at my leisure. One afternoon, I crossed over to a sandbank that had formed in the middle of the river, and was gathering shellfish, intending each one to be the last, when night began to fall and it became impossible to distinguish shells from the stones around them. I stood up to go home when, to my surprise, I saw that the tide had come in and the sandy flats leading up to the riverbank were far off in the distance. The tide was rapidly rising. In the short space of time that I was dithering over what to do, the water had risen and now covered my feet. The thought that I might not make it back across to the riverbank filled me with terror. This was how life was for us children then, full of life-threatening danger that we somehow managed to survive.

---

[64] The monument was originally erected on the site of Hiroshima Castle in 1951. In 1967, after becoming damaged by children who used it as a slingshot target, the monument was moved to Hiroshima Peace Park where it still stands today. It contains an etching of Hara's poem, *Himei* ('Epitaph'), which Bun quotes in the original Japanese in her text.

# Beneath the Sun, Under the Stars

There was no time to reflect on our health problems; our days from dawn to dusk were spent procuring food for the table. Nor was there any room, or need, to worry about what day of the month it was or how many days had passed since the blast. With sunrise, we would commence our activities for survival. Survival activities meant, in effect, activities to stave off starvation. How to procure food for that night's dinner; how to procure food for the following day? We focused all our labors on that, and only that, working until the sun went down.

I can't recall exactly when it was but the first signs of people that I saw on our burned-out plains, were of those who had come from the outskirts of the city, pulling large wagons by hand, to look for items of value among the ruins and take them home. Before long, the wagons had changed to horse-drawn carriages. The *goemon-buro* were considered the most valuable items, it seems. There wasn't a day when the baths didn't vanish and before long the *goemon-buro* in which we had so enjoyed bathing under the star-filled heavens, had all but disappeared. Little by little, people began to return to live amid the ruins. Needless to say, most lived in shacks but there were the occasional people who built real houses with real walls.

We came to know a couple of exceedingly cheerful young men. One was a chap called Tsukamoto, an electrician's son who was very open and broad-minded. The other was Makino, a mild-natured chap who was discreet but not withdrawn. Both had lost their homes in the fires from the blast and were making a living lathing walls. They also gave my brother Mikio, still at junior high then, some part-time work. The young men were greatly impressed with Mikio who was quick to learn the ropes, good at the job, and could get almost twice as much done as the average adult. Every evening they would see Mikio home to

145

our place where they would hungrily devour a few of my mother's steamed sweet potatoes while they chatted about the day's events. The young men always began by telling us of Mikio's escapades – it seemed that not only was Mikio good at the job but he was a great conversationalist and got up to some highly amusing antics. Next, they'd pass on information about others living on the burned plains. It was through them that we learned about people from our neighborhood, Hakushima; who had returned for instance, or was building a house; what happened to such and such at the time of the blast. Every evening, the pair of men would thus spend an entertaining hour or two with us at home, perched on the steps at our entrance.

There was one other thing that excited their interest at our house, the presence of Aunt Tomiko, my older sister Mitsuko, and myself. We three were as close as sisters, despite our disparate personalities and the five years' difference in age between each of us. Indeed, I referred to my aunty as Tomiko-neesan,[65] just as my older sister was Mitsuko-neesan, and still do so now in my eighties. During the daytime, all three of us would be busy working but in the evenings, after dinner, we would go outside and sit down in a row on the fire-ravaged earth where, never lost for conversation, we chatted about all manner of things.

Even in the dark you could sense the vast expanse of the wasteland, while the star-filled night sky seemed to stretch out endlessly. A new moon would appear, a slender arc in the sky like a delicate, golden brushstroke. Several days later, it would have waxed to a radiant crescent the shape of a fine-edged scythe. This would be followed by a celestial harp, then the softly glowing 'thirteenth-night moon', or gibbous moon, before a glorious full moon, breathtakingly large, eventually lit up the sky. Next evening, the waning moon would appear on the horizon, enshrouded in an indescribable sadness. Meeting one's gaze in the distance was the boundless universe.

Those evenings of conversation never centered on health issues or our struggles to survive. On the contrary, we engaged in almost fanciful discussions as we allowed our imaginations

---

[65] *Neesan* is a term of endearment normally used for one's older sisters or for youngish women who are like an older sister.

to soar toward the future. We may well have kept going over similar ground, but our talks were always infused with new hopes and dreams. The two young men, who delighted in letting their imaginations run wild, judged Aunt Tomiko to be a 'woman chasing dreams', Mitsuko a 'pragmatic woman', and me a 'woman of high ideals'.

Little by little, however, the *goemon-buro* disappeared from the city's ravaged plains, survivors began to return to the city, and a semblance of normality started to return to our lives. Tsukamoto had to try to rebuild the family's electrician business. Makino moved in with a woman not much younger than his mother, causing a scandal in the neighborhood and an endless stream of criticism of the woman; "Makino was such a good, honest young man until he fell under that woman's spell!" "She was born in the year of the horse with the heavenly symbol of fire, wasn't she? Just goes to show, the old saying about such women killing their men is true!" "Imagine, at her age, she ought to be ashamed of herself!" "Poor Makino, she's ruined his life!" Open and candid by nature, the woman had enjoyed a wide circle of friends in the neighborhood. Yet as a result of this one incident, she was suddenly condemned as a wicked woman. *But surely love knows no age!* I secretly thought.

# Floating Lanterns in Front of the Atomic Bomb Dome

On the evenings of the fifth and sixth of August, survivors of the blast would walk down to the banks of the Motoyasu River on the Atomic Bomb Dome side of the river, carrying handmade lanterns in shared lamentation.

Whenever that time of the year came around, my family likewise split some fine branches of bamboo and, with some paper and paste, created lanterns. As night fell, we would set out to the Dome in the cool evening breeze, accompanied by grandmother and her family. Our lanterns bore the names of Uncle Torao, Hideo, Ms Tomoyanagi, and later when he passed away, Iida Yoshiaki, handwritten respectively by grandmother, mother, and me. Down at the river, we placed lighted candles in the lanterns and then gently set them afloat on the water where they would linger at arm's reach almost as if they were sad to part from us. Tears rolling down our cheeks, we would gently push them out toward the faster current. At length, the lanterns drifted away from the banks whereupon we would set off along the riverbank with other families of the deceased, trying to keep abreast with the lanterns, as if in pursuit of lost parents, children, and other loved ones.

On one particular occasion, it seemed the tide was to peak in the evening for the lanterns firstly made their way upstream. The sight of the lanterns travelling slowly up the river as if they longed for home, and looking as though the slightest puff of wind or ripple would kill their flame or overturn them, was enough to bring more tears to our eyes. With the turn of the tide, the lanterns huddled together near the banks, the odd one breaking free to bob up and down precariously on the water. These spirits of the dead were transported out to sea, just like on the day of the blast, each suffused with an air of unbearable grief, glowing a mournful blue, or shrill red. Next morning, we were told, Hiroshima's seashore was buried in lifeless lanterns.

At some stage, I don't recall exactly when, an elderly woman began selling simple, handmade lanterns on the bank near the Dome. Hearing that she was living a sad, lonely existence after losing all her children in the blast, we decided to buy our lanterns from her. A few years later, however, she was gone and we never saw her again. When, after a break of several years, I revisited the river to float some lanterns, I found the banks had undergone a complete transformation; gone were the natural shoreline and banks of the past. On the water floated a few lanterns, all of similar shape and design. A person in a boat was using a long pole to push back into the flow any that happened to float toward the banks. Somewhere, someone was loudly reciting Buddhist scriptures. I looked around for a priest then realized that the voice was coming from a tape deck rigged up on a boat on the river. At the foot of the bridge near Hiroshima Peace Park, a travel agency had pitched a large marquee and was selling ready-made lanterns. The lanterns were sold out by the time I arrived and all that remained was a banner with the price flapping in the breeze. Astonished at how expensive they were, I felt a cold, desolate wind blow through my heart.

How hot Hiroshima's summers are!
Wilting in the scorching sun's rays,
heart heavy with scars, unfading with the passage of time.
Summer – oh how I hate to visit Hiroshima in summer!

"Let's meet again on the sixtieth anniversary of the atomic bombing," I promised when I parted with my friend Ole in Norway. And so it was that over the summer of 2005, I stayed in Hiroshima several days in order to meet this lone anti-nuclear, peace activist. I had timed my visit with the NHK Hiroshima Youth Choir's performance of *A Prayer for Water* so that I could participate in NHK's recording of the event for their Overseas Program. Not only did I see Ole as promised, I also met up unexpectedly with old acquaintances from New Zealand and Sweden, and a number of Japanese individuals, among them distant relatives whom I normally struggle to find

149

time to see in my busy schedule. Once more I was forced to acknowledge Hiroshima's tight hold on me.

That summer of 2005, I joined others again in the lantern-floating ceremony. A dedicated area for floating the lanterns had been set up in Peace Park, on the bank opposite the Atomic Bomb Dome. Crowds of people carrying lanterns were there and it took some time to reach the water's edge; Hiroshima was now an international city and so the floating of the lanterns had taken on a festive atmosphere with shades of tourism. Slipping between the crowds, I gently laid my lantern on the surface of the water, hugging my old grief tightly to me.

# Vision of Levee Frescoes and
# Aerial Esplanades

The people of Hiroshima, 'City of Water', lived in harmony with the city's rivers. Wherever we went, there would be a bridge to cross, and we tended to memorize the lie of the city by the names of the rivers and bridges rather than by district names. Crystalline waters, dazzling white sandy banks; as children, we learned our games and also the meaning of danger on the rivers. We would hold boat races as far as this or that bridge, and at school there would be the occasional swimming marathon during physical education class where we had to swim from one bridge to another.

In early spring, when the *ayu* [66] travel upstream for spawning, I often strolled down to Tokiwa Bridge to watch fishers cast the nets. It was always the same chap who came along, net bundled up and slung over his shoulder. The strip of water between Tokiwa Bridge and the steel bridge for the Sanyō Main Trunk Line was his chosen spot for casting his net. Ripples sparkled on the water's surface and, unless you were watching intently, it would be difficult to determine whether the *ayu* had surfaced or it was just the ripples.

I would be watching with bated breath, gaze fixed on the water, when at length amid the sparkling ripples, a couple of small, sleek, slender fish with a touch of color would catch my eye; *ayu!* In their wake would come a whole shoal. The man with the net on his shoulder would swiftly toss the net out wide. How beautiful it looked – a veritable work of art – as, drawing a magnificent arc, it floated down over the water like a gigantic umbrella. But *ayu* are quick and nimble; the net would be

---

[66] Plecoglossus altivelis, or commonly known in English as 'sweetfish' on account of the sweetness of its flesh.

hauled in to find at most two or three *ayu*, and often none at all, caught in it. Undeterred, the man would carefully prepare his net for casting once more. Part of the knack of creating that beautiful arc, I learned, was in the folding of the net. For hours on end I would wait again and again for that wonderful moment when the net would unfold.

At the time of the blast, people fled to the rivers, to the embankment and into the water. Some reached the embankment only to breathe their last. Others, seeking water, were dragged out by the tide. Then there were those who, having survived the blast, built shacks and settled on the embankments. Ever since, the river's water has been dark and cloudy, its shores, a muddy bog.

When they began developing a new city plan for Hiroshima, a city reduced to ashes, we heard of two concepts that were unique for their time. The first one was to turn the area lining both sides of all of the city's rivers into verdant river parks, and to invite painters and sculptors from around the globe to carve frescoes into the levee around the Atomic Bomb Dome. The hope was that this would bring comfort to the survivors and appease the souls of the dead. The other concept was to build several high-rise municipal apartments in Motomachi, a district bordering the river that was now a slum where atomic bomb survivors lived in cramped, crowded conditions; the idea was that these people would move from the shacks to live in the apartments. Any remaining space would be planted in greenery and, at the rooftops connecting the apartment blocks, would be aerial esplanades. For someone like me living in the city's ruins, these two concepts, as visions of the future Hiroshima, fired the imagination.

Neither of these plans was realized.

Today, the banks around Peace Park, which receives many visitors from outside the city, are protected by a concrete levee and an esplanade runs alongside the river, but the area upstream where I used to play as a child is now such a muddy bog I can no longer even picture the crystal-clear waters of the past. What need is there for banks hardened with concrete or an esplanade like an artificial garden? Give us back the crystalline waters and white sandy riverbanks so that the people of Hiroshima can enjoy the water as part of their daily lives, and visitors to the city can dip their hands in the rivers and be filled with a sense of peace and calm in Hiroshima, 'City of Water'.

# Requiem

It was in 1947, as I recall, that summer grasses grew wildly on the ruins of Hiroshima Castle – this after it was rumored that no trees or plants would grow for the next seventy-five years. I find it extraordinary to this day to think that all those people and animals burned in the blast (from the moment the bomb was dropped, and for some time after, all signs of animal life disappeared) perished so fleetingly and helplessly, and yet weeds soon took root in the injured earth and grew rampantly. The survivors picked those weeds to stave off starvation.

That year, in order to earn a regular income to support my family of five – mother, father, younger brother and sister, and me – I started working at sixteen. Had I stayed on, it would have been my last year of schooling under the education system at the time. I think there were only two or three pupils in my grade left at school after we were given permission to graduate a year earlier than usual. One day at work, I caught snatches of someone saying, "At the Castle ruins…a performance…Yamada," or something to that effect. I hurriedly finished my allotted tasks and ran up to the ruins that were less than five minutes' walk away. Nothing was left of the castle after it had been blasted into the moat by the atomic explosion. In the castle gardens, the old military headquarters from the time of the Sino-Japanese War had completely crumbled but escaped the fires after the blast, shielded perhaps by the surrounding moat.

A small group of around twenty chamber musicians had erected makeshift seating in the long grass and, decked out in dazzling white shirts, were giving a performance. As I recall, they were all playing stringed instruments; their haunting tone sounded like the cries of the dead rising up from the depths of the earth – so poignant, so powerful, it stopped me in my tracks. There I stood, entranced, in the long, thick grass. Atop the stone foundations of the military headquarters, the conductor was waving his baton, completely absorbed; sometimes he brought his hands together as if in prayer, other times he waved them about, wildly, tragically, like a flag buffeted by the wind. Seen from the slightly elevated ruins, Hiroshima was a vast expanse of scorched earth the color of umber with absolutely nothing left to obstruct the view. The music rang out passionately, mournfully, its plaintive tones floating over the sea of rubble before being drawn up into the sky as if reaching up toward the souls of those who had risen to heaven on the day of the blast. There was no audience, nor any applause, only this prayer to the heavens and earth. My first ever contact with classical music, I stood motionless in the chest-high grasses, deeply moved. The grasses exuded a warm, damp fragrance and moaned in the wind like living creatures. Even now, I occasionally wake in the night from a strange dream to find myself short of breath and my chest tightly constricted. It amazes me to think that these dreams spring from the requiem that the musicians played on that day many years ago. I wonder whether the conductor called 'Yamada' was the late Yamada Kazuo,[67] or if any of the musicians are still alive and well. How I have longed, for some years now, to meet any that are.

---

[67] 山 田 一 雄　(1912–1991).　Famous 20th-century Japanese composer and conductor.

# Two Cenotaphs

Twenty or so years ago, I had the opportunity to visit Hawaii. Early one morning, I strolled down to the harbor, a place I had long wished to see. A gale was blowing that day, whipping up the waves. Visible amid the chop offshore was the white cenotaph erected in memory of those who died in the Pearl Harbor Attack. Before heading there, we were shown a film featuring the valiant Japanese army, a close-up of the Shōwa Emperor[68] on horseback, and footage of the surprise attack on Pearl Harbor (some say that it wasn't a surprise and there is strong evidence to support them; it is an established fact, for instance, that the United States had broken the Japanese army's secret code and was keeping a record of their movements. If that is indeed the case, it would suggest that Hawaii was sacrificed by the American government for political ends).

The film over, we boarded boats in groups of around twenty to thirty people and made our way out to the white edifice floating on the water offshore. The complex stands over the battle ship, USS Arizona, providing an excellent view from its terrace of the sunken ship's exterior. A slick of oil still floats on the water around the ship's large funnel that juts up above the sea's surface, and we were told that the bodies of the dead seamen lie submerged inside the ship's rusty interior; they've been resting there for more than half a century now – pecked and nibbled at by fish over the years, they are surely no longer recognizable. I shuddered at the thought of my own sons resting there underfoot and wondered why, after all this time, the bodies would be left in a ship lying in such shallow water so close to shore. All I could see was the foolishness of the power

---

[68] Emperor Hirohito (1901–1989) reigned from 1926 until his death in 1989.

mongers, American rulers, who justify war and incite people into battle. Was I mistaken?

Gorgeous flowers adorned the cenotaph. I stood before it for some time, gazing at the names of the dead etched on its façade. And in my mind, though I knew them not, I spoke to each of the dead soldiers, spoke to them as a fellow human.

In Hiroshima's Peace Memorial Park, there is likewise a cenotaph, fashioned in stone after the ancient clay Haniwa houses. The cenotaph is inscribed with the epitaph, 'Rest in peace, the error shall never be repeated.' The epitaph represents an apology from the people of the twentieth century for committing the evil of war, the greatest crime against humanity, and the atrocity of exploding an atomic bomb on fellow human beings. And it makes the pledge that such foolishness will never be repeated.

Flowers adorn the memorial in Hiroshima too. But they are not elaborate bouquets like those placed before the memorial in Hawaii by the US Navy. These are small, meager bunches placed there by ordinary people as an expression of love and compassion. For me, the different messages that these two cenotaphs convey are a cause for profound reflection.

Whenever I return to Hiroshima I head down to the cenotaph. Once there, the sight of a certain object fluttering high, just slightly off to the side, behind the monument invariably makes me feel deeply despondent; it is the Japanese *Hinomaru*, or 'Rising sun' flag, with its distinctive red disk against a white background. For most Japanese people, especially ordinary people of my generation, the *Hinomaru* symbolizes war. The *Hinomaru* flag was waved to incite people to war, and we waved *Hinomaru* flags when we sent our soldiers off to the front. Under the *Hinomaru* flag, our soldiers invaded other countries, killing their citizens and dying themselves, until eventually, the atomic bomb was dropped on us. Scores of foreigners also perished when the bomb was dropped on Hiroshima, including some American prisoners of war.

Many foreigners visit Hiroshima. I wonder how they feel when they see the Japanese *Hinomaru* flag fluttering in the breeze near the memorial. There is an internationally recognized, anti-nuclear peace emblem. Surely that would

157

make a much more suitable flag for Hiroshima? And then there's the monument erected in memory of the hundreds of thousands of Korean people who are said to have perished in the blast. This has been erected on another site in the Peace Memorial Park. I fail to understand why they don't have the one memorial for all those that perished.

After farewelling my mother from this world, I put into action my plan to travel the world promoting peace. Nearly seventy years old by then, I traveled around numerous countries, sometimes up to eight or nine countries a year, learning many things, and having many precious encounters with people. These travels enlightened me on the nature of 'national character'. A month's stay in Central America, followed one year later by a three-week journey to the Arctic region, made me aware of the huge differences in national character. I imagine that a country's geographical location on the globe, its climate, and centuries of human habitation combine to cultivate certain national traits. In which case, the gods have favored the Japanese people by giving them the best-positioned land on earth, a land that is neither severely cold nor mercilessly hot. This small island nation, surrounded by sea in all four directions of the compass, is blessed with rich forests, clean water, wonderful seafood and delicacies to be had from the land; it is a rich, fertile region for creating and nurturing life. Additionally, I believe the subtle changes of the four seasons have also greatly affected Japanese culture and our national character. We Japanese need to acknowledge and be grateful for these things.

Japan should become a haven for the world by building a country that fulfills its constitution's peace mission. As an aside, my eldest son who graduated from university during Japan's period of high economic growth[69] told me that he wrote his graduating thesis on turning Japan into a medical mecca. In those days after the atomic blast, as we struggled to survive in a city of death with nothing but rubble for as far as the eye could

---

[69] Japan experienced high economic growth most especially during the period from the mid-1950s to the 1970s but the economy remained buoyant well into the 1980s when Bun's son will have graduated.

see, I wished for peace with all my heart, and for the elimination not only of war but of all those conditions that threaten the very foundations of human life, such as starvation, disease, and discrimination. Most of the survivors of the atomic blast personally experienced all of these conditions. They say that our 'peace constitution' is built on our experience of the atomic bombing of Hiroshima and Nagasaki. So what has the Japanese government been doing since our defeat in the Pacific War? "We are the only country in the world to have suffered a nuclear attack," they say, seemingly filled with a strong sense of righteousness. Yet do they really know what it means to suffer from the effects of nuclear weapons? Do they truly understand not just the misery immediately following the blast, but also what it means to suffer the effects of radiation poisoning for the rest of one's life?

The nuclear threat, furthermore, doesn't simply come from nuclear bombs but includes ongoing nuclear tests, nuclear power plant accidents, nuclear waste disposal and workers' exposure to radiation at nuclear power plants. When operating, nuclear power plants continually release small amounts of radiation. This pollutes the sea, air, and land, and is absorbed by us internally via these. In time, this may bring about the demise of all living things on earth. If the government reflected fully on this, could it keep touting the notion of Japan being 'the only country in the world to have suffered a nuclear attack'? Not likely! While repeating this refrain, the Japanese government frequently abstains when a vote is taken at international anti-nuclear conventions.

Japan is a small country with few natural resources. There is no need for us to become a superpower, or to compete with other countries in order to achieve this. Only when Japan aims to be a truly peaceful nation in line with its constitution will we be welcomed and loved by the rest of the world.[70] I believe that

---

[70] Japan's post-war constitution is known as the 'Peace Constitution' for its unequivocal renunciation of war and the threat or use of force as a means of settling international disputes. For a full English translation of the constitution see:
http://japan.kantei.go.jp/constitution_and_government_of_japan/constitution_e.html

this is the only path for Japan to follow. If, along the way, the United States and other nuclear nations apply pressure to Japan, then, and only then, can Japan proudly and justly say, "We are the only nation to have suffered from a nuclear attack." Until then, I'd rather those words were sealed away.

Rest in peace, the error shall never be repeated," says the epitaph inscribed on the cenotaph in Hiroshima's Peace Memorial Park. I would like Japan's rulers to reflect deeply on those words.

# Ms. Tomoyanagi

On that fateful morning of August 6, when I was injured in the atomic blast, it was Ms. Tomoyanagi, from the Savings Bureau where I worked under the student mobilization scheme, who took me to the Red Cross Hospital, and she was the one who desperately called me back from the brink of death every time I began drifting off. I had lost an enormous amount of blood and doubt I would be alive today were it not for her.

Every month or so, the Savings Bureau would hold an abacus competition for staff which we students could also go along to watch. Ms. Tomoyanagi won hands down every time. She must have been around twenty-three or four at the time; a quiet, retiring person, who would ever have guessed that she was such an expert at abacus? It came about, exactly how I'm unsure, that, having been assigned to the same division as Ms. Tomoyanagi, I would spend lunch breaks learning abacus from her. The idea was to flick the beads of the abacus with the fingers of the right hand while simultaneously flipping over the pages of a thick wad of deposit and withdrawal slips with the left as you added up the figures.

Being a novice, I struggled at first to get my left and right hand working independently but Ms. Tomoyanagi taught me well and with a multitude of practice sheets to learn from at each level, I rapidly improved. Ms. Tomoyanagi would time me. "You've broken my record!" she exclaimed on one occasion with a twinkle in her eye. "What a shame students can't take part in the competition." She was very pleased for me. This is the sort of person Ms. Tomoyanagi, my lifesaver, was.

I wonder how many hours she sat at my side, watching over me, on the day of the blast. I can still hear as clear as day the sound of her crying when, relieved to see that I'd pulled through, she burst into tears, and then the patter of her departing footsteps and voice repeating the words, "I'll definitely be back so please don't move from here," as she left to check on her mother's safety. I only saw Ms. Tomoyanagi once more after that. I was walking along the road through the scorched fields in the direction of Hiroshima Station on some errand or other. Bar this one white, unbroken line, the city was nothing but rubble for as far as the eye could see. Not another pedestrian was in sight until suddenly, from the opposite direction, I spotted a man on a bicycle racing toward me. *A bicycle?* I stopped short in disbelief; at that time those of us living on the blackened plains would get around on foot, our feet bare, and dressed in rags. All we had were the clothes on our backs. The bicycle went flying past with someone on the back. Just as it passed, I heard a cry and a woman call my name. It was Ms. Tomoyanagi! I ran for a short distance after the bicycle calling out her name but, perched on the bicycle's rear carrier, she quickly disappeared from view.

I never forgot Ms. Tomoyanagi. In 1947, two years after the blast, I found employment at the Hiroshima Communications Bureau, having graduated from women's college under the old education system. I was employed by the Ministry of Communications, like Ms. Tomoyanagi; however, the Communications Bureau was in Hakushima while the Savings Bureau, where she worked, was some distance away in Senda-machi. I longed to see her but I had a paralyzing fear of the Savings Bureau; the mere thought of the Bureau brought vivid memories of the horrific scenes at the time of the blast flooding back, making me tremble all over. On bad days, simply facing south in the direction of the Savings Bureau was enough to make me feel dizzy and throw up.

There weren't the phones then as there are nowadays; whenever we needed to make contact with the Savings Bureau over some or other business matter, we would go in person. One day, I asked a male colleague who was going on an errand to the Savings Bureau to pass on a couple of messages to Ms. Tomoyanagi; firstly, to convey my gratitude for her help on the day of the blast, and secondly, to advise her that I was now working at the Communications Bureau. I was unprepared for his reply; "Ms. Tomoyanagi passed away last year from atomic-bomb sickness." *That can't be true! I don't believe it,* I thought but deep inside I turned cold with fear. As far as I recalled, Ms. Tomoyanagi suffered no injuries on the day of the blast, and she had looked well when she passed me on the road that day, perched on the back of a bicycle. I determined to go and check for myself. But I couldn't overcome my fear of the Savings Bureau. Some time passed. I was battling Erythematodes, a type of collagen disease, as discussed earlier, that affected my whole body and for which there was no cure. Eventually, when the disease worsened, I left Hiroshima for treatment.

Thirty years passed.

Once my illness abated, I married in Tokyo and became a mother to three sons. In summer, during the children's school holidays, I sometimes took them back to Hiroshima to visit family. One summer, I decided to take my sons to the Peace Memorial Ceremony for what would also be my very first time. At just after eight in the morning on the day of the ceremony, it was already hot and humid, typical of Hiroshima in summer. A large crowd of people had gathered in the Peace Memorial Park and the air swirled with excitement – it was at the height, perhaps, of the anti-nuclear weapons movement? A grassy area had been cordoned off for survivors of the blast where, in contrast, aged survivors sat all around me with heads bent and a sad air hovering over them as if they were weighed down by immense sorrow. As the ceremony progressed, they began to cry and here and there arose the sound of sobbing. Honored guests gave eulogies and laid flowers at the memorial but it all seemed hollow and meaningless to me.

Once the ceremony was over, my eldest son, a primary school student at the time, asked, "Mother, where were you when the bomb exploded? I'd like to go there. And I want to walk along the same route that you walked." We headed across Heiwa Ōhashi Bridge, and began walking southwards along the tram route in the direction of the Savings Bureau. Though the route itself hadn't changed since the blast, new buildings now lined the road on both sides. I walked in silence. We passed the City Council building then turned left off the tram route at Takanohashi. It was around that time that my legs began to turn to lead. In due course, we came to the Red Cross Hospital. On deciding to go in, I felt a stab of pain in my chest.

The rounded, well-manicured shrubbery in the front garden was still there, looking exactly as it did on the day of the blast but the bare patch of garden leading down to the barren, burned-out fields had been paved over and was now hemmed in by houses built up all around it. I headed straight to one section of the hedge, to the spot where Iida and I had spent the night together huddled under a sheet as the fires roared overhead and sparks rained down on us. I was sure that the crackling in our ears at the time had been the sound of pine leaves burning but now cycads, magnificent specimens with large crowns of leaves, stood in their place.

We went into the hospital waiting room. In the spacious interior, sat orderly rows of chairs filled with patients waiting to pay their medical bill or receive medication. There, in the center of the room, stood the pillar at the base of which, I think, Ms. Tomoyanagi had lain me down. "She's in a bad way, and losing a lot of blood. If you let her sleep, she'll die!" The sounds of a military doctor's voice, departing footsteps, and Ms. Tomoyanagi desperately calling my name, came flooding back to mind. People had lain everywhere sprawled across this floor, on the brink of death. I stood there, motionless, overwhelmed with emotion. Someone sitting on a bench offered me a seat. "Thank you," I said but my legs had a life of their own; they took me toward the basement. When I reached the top of the stairs leading down to the basement, I was suddenly filled with dread and my legs began to shake but I pushed on, slowly descending one step at a time. The basement was now a dining room. *Was that the spot over by the back wall*, I wondered, *where I'd been laid down? Was that where I'd waited for impending death while gazing at the smoke billowing in? And what about the mirror?* I was sure the mirror had been to the right of the staircase but all that was there now were a table and some chairs. There was no mirror.

I headed back outside. The area between the Red Cross Hospital and the Savings Bureau was now completely built up. It was impossible to imagine the flames shooting up from the bare earth on the day of the blast. We arrived at the Savings Bureau. "I was here, inside this building, when the bomb

164

exploded," I said to my sons. "I was near the window on the third floor…" As I explained this to them, I stared dazedly at the ground at my feet; my head felt as heavy as lead, my body numb as if under a spell – I couldn't raise my eyes to look at them.

I visited the Savings Bureau on another three occasions after that, at times when I'd returned to Hiroshima for the children's summer holidays or for family memorial services. Each time I went alone. On the first occasion, I automatically headed to the Bureau's side entrance. Once there, however, I came to a halt and, unable to go any further, ended up retracing my steps. The second time, I managed to make it through the side entrance. Though terrified, I slowly and deliberately made my way up the back staircase, taking one step at a time. *Could those splotches on the wall be someone's bloodstains from the day of the blast?* At the thought, a wave of fear washed over me. I neared the third floor. It was around here that Yuki-chan, the cleaner's daughter, had lain with her abdomen ripped open. At length, I made it to the office on the third floor and went in. The spacious interior was sectioned off into smaller units by means of bookcases and other such furniture. My desk had been in the north-east corner of the room; there was no sign of a desk there now. I briefly explained my story to an employee seated at a desk near the entrance and asked after Ms. Tomoyanagi. "That's a good forty years ago and this is now a branch of the City Council," he kindly explained. "The Savings Bureau shifted to Hiroshima Station into the new government building that was erected at the bullet train terminus. Please enquire there." I thanked him and left but didn't have the courage to go to the new Bureau.

On the third occasion, I went back to visit the old building in order to confirm one of my memories of the blast; I recalled catching sight of the city through a window as I descended the back staircase. I was certain that I had seen firstly the houses in the districts to the left, followed by those to the right, collapse like a pack of cards. The window, as I recalled, was on the second-floor landing but I couldn't remember its exact position and that was what I now wanted to ascertain. I felt deeply shocked and something akin to anger when I found the old Savings Bureau building fenced off by high sheeting and in the process of being demolished. Printed on the fence were the words 'Fujita-gumi', the company founded by mother's Uncle Ichirō. I circled the fence many times. It was a Sunday and the entrance to the worksite was closed. A yellow crane lifted its curved, sickle-like neck toward the clouds. Unable to pull myself away, I peered through a tiny gap in the fence. Inside, I saw the building had already been half destroyed, exposing a ghastly gaping wound. Crane's claws gripped a lump of broken concrete. I felt as though the large, dirty talons were clawing at my heart and imagined I heard a roar as something precious, something irreplaceable, began crumbling inside me. At the same time, however, I could feel the slow but sure melting away of the 'Savings Bureau phobia' that had lain in my heart for so long.

After that, I made my way to the Savings Bureau's new building, a modern building the likes of which could be found anywhere but which was completely new to me. I felt calm and composed when I saw it. The woman at the reception said gently, "We've been getting a number of people like yourself lately, looking for people who were employed here at the time of the blast. Let me check the old registers in storage. I'll get back to you once I have more information."

Several days later, the results of her search arrived in the mail. Apparently, Ms. Tomoyanagi and her sister were both employed at the Savings Bureau at the time. It seems that the Tomoyanagi I knew was the younger of the two. "Her position terminated with her death in 1946," said the letter. So it was true, she had indeed passed away. Her death, the possibility of which had troubled me for many years, was now a sad fact, lodged firmly in my heart. With this realization, I began to search for her older sister. I asked my cousin living in Hiroshima to look into it for me but he said he hadn't a clue where to start as the layout of the city, and the names of the areas, had changed after the war. I was ready to admit defeat when my cousin sent news of a woman living in a home for the elderly on the outskirts of Hiroshima, apparently Ms. Tomoyanagi's older sister, although she was known by another name. "Her mental health may not be good, I suggest you address any correspondence to the nurse," he advised but I received no reply to my letter.

He must have been mistaken about her.

In August, 1994, I had taken my mother, who by then was living with me and my family in Kamakura, back to Hiroshima for a family memorial service. We stayed at the home of one of my aunts. One evening when we were eating dinner, the phone rang. "I'm Tomoyanagi Toshiko's older sister," the voice at the other end of the receiver said. "I rang your home in Kamakura but was told that you were in Hiroshima and redirected here." It seemed that she was a different person from the one living in the home for the elderly. "Please forget about my sister and stop your searching," she pleaded. Lost for words, I made no response. "I'm all alone now and don't want to remember the past. Just making this phone call brings tears to my eyes even after all these years. Please forget my sister." I began to cry with her. "I live in Misasa," she said but refused to give me her address and phone number, or even to tell me where her sister's grave was, no matter how many times I asked. Though deeply hurt, I realized then that there are people, even now, whose wounds are still open and raw. Half a century passed before I was finally able to write about the atomic bombing of Hiroshima; if asked, I can now talk about my experiences. But the phone call from Ms. Tomoyanagi's older sister reminded me once more that the terrifying experiences of the atomic bomb are not something of the past; some fifty years later, they remain fresh as ever in people's minds.

# Mr. Iida

That night under the roaring inferno, as sparks rained down on us, I came back from the brink of death and spent a peaceful night – uncannily peaceful – with Iida Yoshiaki. He had walked, wounded, among the dying, and stopped to give each and every one a drink of water. Now he too is no longer of this world. From that morning of the eighth of August, when we parted at the foot of Miyuki Bridge, not a day went by when I didn't think of him. I wanted at least to thank him. After the blast, my family continued to have a close association with the Murai family, who were his relatives he said. On one occasion, I asked them about him only to be told, "From what we understand, the Iida boy is a delinquent, a good-for-nothing, who spends his time with his head stuck in books and listening to Western music, of all things, in this day and age!" Back then, 'delinquent' was a label young men and women tried to avoid at all costs. Feeling that his name had been sullied, I never again spoke of him to the Murais.

Earlier I wrote about finding employment in 1947 with the Hiroshima Communications Bureau. For survivors of the atomic bomb, repatriates and ex-servicemen in Hiroshima, every single day was a struggle and they harbored little hope for the future. Employees at the Communications Bureau were likewise perpetually hungry, tired and downcast. Not so the administration section to which I was assigned. It published a monthly magazine titled *Aozora* (Blue Skies) with the motto 'Forever bright, fun and young'. Everyone, senior staff members and new recruits alike, were to contribute to the magazine. A young returned serviceman by the name of Mr. Yuuki single-handedly saw to everything, the planning, editing, printing on the mimeograph, and even the distribution of the magazine. He was like the sun, lighting up our section, a large department with a big staffing establishment from the Chief of the Bureau at the very top, right down to the janitor. In addition to publishing *Aozora*, Mr. Yuuki retrieved his books from the countryside where he'd sent them for safe-keeping and circulated them among staff, and he encouraged Bureau employees and Hiroshima University students to contribute to a haiku magazine titled *Yakeno* (Burned Fields) that he edited and published. The haiku magazine grew to include contributions from Ministry of Communications staff nationwide.

Mr. Yuuki also organized an annual drama festival in which every department and section of the Bureau performed a play. There were even prizes like a block of soap or a towel – all valuable items at the time – for the best performances. The year after I joined the Bureau, our section put on a performance of Miyazawa Kenji's 'Poran no hiroba' (Poran's Square) [71] at the drama festival. Mr. Yuuki oversaw the planning and directing while almost everyone else in the section participated as actors or stagehands. I was a village maiden, along with a large group of female staff members; our role was to sing and dance.

A woman chosen as music director, instructed us on the singing. Later, I realized that the melody was 'Ode to Joy' from Beethoven's ninth symphony. Even now, whenever I hear 'Ode to Joy', the lyrics from Miyazawa Kenji's 'Poran no hiroba', fall from my lips.

I will never forget the day before the performance; several of the other female employees and I went to gather clover growing wildly on the city's burned-out ruins for wreathing into garlands to adorn our 'village maidens' hair. One of the women sang 'Lorelei', 'Niwa no chigusa' (Garden plants), 'Hanyū no yado' (Hovel), and 'Bodaiju' (Linden tree) for us as she picked. Her beautiful, clear tones took my breath away and I was mesmerized by the mellifluous Western songs, the first

---

[71] Miyazawa Kenji (宮沢賢治; 1896–1933) is a famous Japanese poet, writer, and educator. 'Poran no hiroba' is one of only four plays written by Miyazawa. First performed in 1924, it received scant attention during Miyazawa's lifetime and wasn't published until after his death.

I'd ever heard. Our 'Poran no hiroba' was selected unanimously by the judges for first prize. *Aozora* put out a special edition titled *Poran no hiroba*, for which I wrote a composition called 'The Village Maiden, Fumi'. Not surprisingly, the following year we decided to tackle another of Miyazawa Kenji's works, 'Guskō Budori no denki' (The Life of Guskō Budori).[72] I was selected for one of the major parts, the young woman for whom Budori harbored romantic feelings (his younger sister in the original). 'Budori' and I were given special training sessions over lunch break and after work where we rehearsed in front of Mr. Yuuki and several of the stagehands. It was the first time I had worked closely with Mr. Yuuki and I found him rather intimidating; he was very demanding and had the ability to read one's mind.

"I'm going to take some of the students from my old junior high school to the mountains. Would you like to come too?" he said on another occasion, inviting me and a number of other colleagues. Once again, I was enlisted to write an essay on the trip for inclusion in a collection of essays that he was editing titled *Yamagusa* (Mountain grasses). It was a beautiful clear day and the fresh mountain air was like an elixir for us, physically and spiritually exhausted as we were from the daily grind. Having found the floating clouds soothing, I wrote an essay titled, 'Clouds'.

Suddenly, the energetic Mr. Yuuki was diagnosed with tuberculosis. He had to take time off work and recuperate at home. When after several months he returned to work, I ran into him in the corridor and he enquired, "Do you know Mr. Iida?"

"Mr. Iida? Do you mean Iida Yoshiaki?" Mr. Yuuki proceeded to tell me how Mr. Iida was a friend from junior high, a couple of years his junior, and happened to drop by while he was at home receiving treatment. Mr. Yuuki apparently related to his school friend how he had revived the

---

[72] One of Miyazawa's famous novellas, *Guskō Budori no denki* is also one of the few works published during his lifetime. It was originally published in the literary magazine *Jidō Bungaku* (Children's Literature) in 1932. A 1994 animated movie adaptation was remade by Sujii Gisaburō to much acclaim in 2012.

mountain climbing club and published *Mountain Grasses*. Iida had been listening while flicking through the collection of essays with an air of nostalgia when his hand abruptly stopped mid-air. "What's the matter?"

"I know this person," he had said, recognizing my name – we had exchanged names while we sheltered from the raging inferno. "Please let me see Iida," I pleaded. "He's been constantly on my mind. I want to at least say a word of thanks to him."

"Sure, I'll arrange a meeting sometime." Several days, possibly even months, passed. One day, Tomio, an old childhood friend of mine, dropped by. Although his family was now living with his maternal grandparents on an island in the Seto Inland Sea after evacuating there following the atomic blast, Tomio, who was working at Hiroshima University, was boarding in Hiroshima. Sometimes nostalgia would draw him back to Hakushima. On that particular day, he joined us for an evening meal as he was wont to do. While eating he said, "One of my friends is such a great guy. He sits next to me at work, goes by the name of Iida."

"Did you say Iida? You don't mean Iida Yoshiaki, do you?"

"Good heavens! How is it that you know him Fumi-chan?" And so it happened that Tomio arranged for the two of us to meet well before Mr. Yuuki got around to it. There was a café on the second floor of a building diagonally opposite Fukuya Department Store in the central city. Iida and I sat facing each other across a table there next to the window. We were both deeply moved. The scar from the wound to his forehead was only faintly visible. I managed to wheedle him into unbuttoning his shirtfront so that I could see the scar on his chest. When I told him that I'd been seeking his whereabouts for the last five years, he remarked that he hadn't attempted to look for me. "I wanted to remember you as you were that day."

We were both struggling to survive. There were no phones, and public transportation wasn't convenient like it is today. Iida visited me at home several times but he was a very quiet, reserved person and never stayed for dinner with us. We would take a quiet stroll and that was it. One day, he invited me to go yachting. It was a fine midsummer's day without a cloud in the sky. In the strong wind, the small yacht with its bright white sails sped across the water. "Hold on tight to the mast!" he cautioned, his words scattering in the wind, as he gripped the rudder. The yacht tilted so sharply that its side almost touched the water. I clung to the mast for dear life. The sky and sea were a deep blue; a jubilant, breathtaking blue glimpsed in the midst of our miserable post-atomic blast life. "Did you enjoy that?" Iida asked after we disembarked, looking me straight in the eye for the first time.

That was to be the last time I saw Iida.

As related earlier, I was afflicted with an intractable disease – whether connected to my being exposed to the bomb, I know not – and the symptoms were particularly bad at that time. On the recommendation of Dr. Hachiya, the Director of Hiroshima Communications Bureau Hospital, I was accepted as a patient at Tokyo Communications Bureau Hospital. While there I had a close encounter with death but eventually pulled through and my condition improved considerably. Whenever I returned to Hiroshima, however, the symptoms would worsen and I'd find myself back in hospital in Tokyo. This went on for several years until, on the doctor's advice, I asked the Bureau for a transfer to Tokyo. Not long after that I received a letter from Tomio. "Iida has passed away. He died in a traffic accident, leaving a young son behind. It's a great loss."

Ms. Tomoyanagi had already passed away, or so I'd heard; I hadn't yet checked for myself. From then on, I kept asking myself, was it acceptable for me to be alive and doing nothing when the two people who had saved me from the brink of death had passed away? Yet the very thought of the bomb sent a chill through me, making me shy away from the topic. Every year when August 6 came around, I would feel as if a heavy weight were bearing down on my shoulders and pass the day in desperately low spirits.

Caught up in the daily grind, almost half a century passed before finally I was able to write poems on the bombing and to talk about it when asked. I set about tracking down Iida's family. Eventually, the same year that I received the phone call from Ms. Tomoyanagi's sister, I learned the whereabouts of Iida's wife and son. And, in August 1994, when I returned to Hiroshima for the fiftieth anniversary memorial services for my

172

uncle and younger brother, I went with Iida's wife and son to visit his grave. The Iida family grave lies in Hiroshima at the foot of Mt. Mitaki. Iida's father died at sea, his younger sister and brother from the atomic blast. His younger sister was fourteen years old, his younger brother, seven – the same ages as me and my younger brother Hideo at the time of the blast. Iida's wife told me that his mother regretted to the end of her days the fact that she wasn't there at the side of a single member of her family to watch over them as they departed from this world.

On the day of the blast, Iida's younger brother Susumu, who was a primary school first-grader, left for school in the morning with the words, *itte kimāsu* (see you later). They never found his body. Iida's mother never accepted her younger son's death, no matter how many years or decades passed. On the day of the blast, she stood on a bridge over the Ōta River that took countless dead bodies out to sea, and called his name time and time again. Later, whenever a new phonebook came out, she would look up all the names listed with the reading 'Iida Susumu' – for she figured that her son was only a young boy at the time of the blast and may have forgotten the Sino-Japanese characters for his name, or that he may still be alive but has lost his memory. Dialing a number, she would say, "Excuse me, you wouldn't happen to be….?"

"I'm so sorry but I think you have the wrong number," the person at the other end of the receiver would say apologetically whereupon she would feel greatly disheartened before rallying and dialing the next number on the list. This apparently continued until almost the day she died. As for Iida, his wife told me that his mother sometimes said to people she was talking to, "My older son is currently overseas." No doubt she struggled to come to terms with his death when he had safely survived the blast.

Five tombstones lined up in a row, all that was left to tell the story of the parents and their three children.

"*Mizuhiki* plants[73] grow in clusters here," commented Iida's wife as I followed her. We made our way into the damp,

---

[73] Persicaria filiformis. A type of Jumpseed with small pink and white flowers reminiscent of the fine red and white thread called

northern side of the mountain. *Mizuhiki*; as a child, I used to love their somewhat forlorn flowers. I was overcome with nostalgia as I recalled Iida's quiet, reserved temperament. Apparently, he didn't say much to his family about the blast. His wife, son, and I spent the day together like old friends, piecing together Iida's younger years with his life after he married. In the room housing the Iida family altar,[74] sat a large, solitary antique speaker. The wooden frame was covered in Gobelin tapestry cloth, the embroidery stunning, though worn. "There's not much room in this house so I'd been thinking of throwing it out," said his wife who had only moved there several days before. "But my husband took such good care of it. He had been talking about having the cover redone in the same design but, as it turns out, he....," she began before breaking off.

After the war, there was just one café along Hiroshima's Nagaregawa Road that played music. It was called Mushika. Though not particularly large, it had an open fire opposite the entrance and, to the right of the fireplace was a counter where they poured you coffee and took requests for the next record. It had a wonderful ambience with soft candle light – or was it lamps that they used? – and a peaceful air. It was at this café that I first heard Tchaikovsky's violin concerto; it almost moved me to tears. *I'd love to become a violinist*, I thought, *so that I might play this piece.* Then the piano concerto by the same composer thrilled me and again I thought I'd love to become a pianist in order to play it. *What dreams!* Yet I seriously entertained these thoughts. It was at this café that I was introduced one by one to the major classical works by Beethoven, Brahms, Mozart, and the like. Over a cup of coffee, I would wait for them to play my request. I always sat in the same spot, a chair in the corner under the stairs. It may be that

---

'mizuhiki' that is used to decorate wedding cards, wrapping and the like on celebratory occasions in Japan, hence its name.

[74] Many Japanese families have a Buddhist altar in the home. It commonly serves as a site for communing with deceased family members and ancestors whom it enshrines, conveying the latest news, praying for the repose of the dead and so forth, rather than for praying to Buddha as such.

Iida had also been seated somewhere at Mushika, listening to the same music at the same time on the very same evenings as me because the speaker with the Gobelin tapestry cover turned out to be one of the speakers from that café and he was apparently a regular customer. His wife told me that when the café was closed down, the manager and Iida decided that they would each take home a speaker. Iida's wife gave me his self-portrait adorning the altar. "My husband already had this painting at the time that we married. It's probably closest of all his paintings to the time when you knew him."

After the war, I briefly attended night classes at an art school. My father and mother were opposed to the idea at the time – it was unheard of for a young woman to go out at night to art classes – however, because one of our neighbor's sons happened to be a teacher at the school, they eventually relented. I was interested in art history but no matter how hard I tried, cast drawing was simply not my forte. The petite, elderly teacher with his characteristic beret was a real gentleman and always praised my work but I wasn't convinced. Then a letter came from the school, addressed to my father. "Your daughter isn't posing as a nude model, is she?" it said. It wasn't me posing nude. Nevertheless, having overextended myself financially and time-wise to attend classes, I used this incident as an opportunity to quit. Apparently, Iida had been attending night classes at the same art school around the same time as me. After I finished my sketching for the evening, I would head home, passing through the lounge where the life drawing group was studying. Sometimes, I stopped briefly to admire their skillful artwork. Had Iida been a member of that group? He apparently continued to paint throughout his life. The many sketches that his wife showed me revealed the depth of his learning but it was clear that his real passion had been oil painting.

While I was still living in Hiroshima, I used to compose haiku, and so, it seemed, did Iida. We were in different groups but when I was shown a posthumous collection of his haiku, it was clear that he was from the same haiku school and I was familiar with the name of the person who had made the selection for the collection. There was a time too when I loved dropping in to antique shops for a browse, and was interested in pottery. After the children had grown up, I had been considering asking for lessons from a potter in Seto[75] but she passed away before I had the chance to do so. Apparently, Iida had a similar interest in antiques and pottery. "The only thing that stopped him from becoming a collector, it would seem, was the lack of money," his wife said as she gave me a Shino-ware sake cup.[76] "When he came back after acquiring this," she added, "he lay face down in bed and held it in the palm of his hand, fondling it endlessly."

To this day, I have never acquired the skills to paint, write haiku, or make pottery. By contrast it seems that in his short life of thirty-seven years, Iida acquired a deep knowledge of all of these arts. Sometimes, on the evening of the sixth of August, I overlay my image of his face reflected in the golden light of the inferno onto his self-portrait, painted on a small piece of plywood in ruddy hues. And I reflect on how I would like to live my life in a similar fashion to Iida on the night of the blast, quietly and with a steadfast love of humanity.

---

[75] A town near Nagoya.

[76] Shino-yaki. Originally from Mino Province, present day Gifu Prefecture, Shino-yaki is said to have developed in the 16th century. It has a characteristic creamy white glaze with red tints and a rough, pitted texture.

# Later Events in My Life

In spring of 1997, I accompanied the NHK Hiroshima Youth Choir on their Italian concert tour. My poem, *Genbaku-ki* (Atomic Bomb Lament), had been set to music by Kihara Kiyotoshi[77] and was on the program. I was heartened to see how the anti-nuclear, peace message conveyed in the songs the children sang had the power to move the hearts of people in other lands. One evening at the very end, as I recall, of the concert tour, the adults spent a few pleasurable hours relaxing in the bar. Everyone being from Hiroshima, the topic of conversation naturally turned to the atomic blast. I was relaying my experiences on that fateful morning, and was just explaining how I had heard the doctor at the Red Cross Hospital say, "She's losing an awful amount of blood. Don't let her sleep or she'll die," and then Ms. Tomoyanagi calling my name, when Dr. Yamazaki, the doctor accompanying the Choir exclaimed, "I think that was my father!" Apparently, his father was Director of the Dental Department at the Red Cross Hospital back then and on duty that morning as Air Raid Commander and Leader of the Fire-Fighting Squad. After I returned to Japan, I was eager to meet Dr. Yamazaki's father, to show him that I was alive and well and thank him but we lived far apart, he in Western Japan, me in the east. He passed away on the May 17th, 1999, before I could realize those wishes.

In 2001, when I returned to Hiroshima for the memorial service on the occasion of the third anniversary of my mother's death, I was able to visit Dr. Yamazaki's father's grave with his family. There was a cozy air about the grave, glistening in the soft rain, and I was filled with deep emotion as I stood before his headstone and communed with him. It was in Peace

---

[77] 木原宏寿: Composer. Born in Hiroshima in 1963.

Cemetery on the mountain slopes in Koi. Just to the north, in Mt. Mitaki graveyard, lay Iida Yoshiaki's grave. Ms. Tomoyanagi's grave may also lie somewhere in the vicinity. One never knows, someday, I may also manage to meet up with Ms. Tomoyanagi.

Though afflicted with an intractable disease, I managed to survive. At thirty I married and while still in my thirties, was blessed with three sons. But then in my forties, my symptoms once again took a turn for the worse and the doctor advised that I may only have half a year left to live. Having faced death several times before, I took this in my stride. Nevertheless, I was deeply concerned for my three young sons. I thought, *I want to leave them something to remember me by*. I had been in a haiku group, composing poetry for a decade from around the time I turned twenty. A senior member in the group at the time presided over a coterie magazine that published poems intended to be set to music and sung. This gave me the idea of writing lyrics for a children's song so that whenever the going got tough, my sons could hum my song and find in it the strength to carry on.

Ten years passed. I had managed to live on. I decided to collect the poems that I had written as a message to my children over the last decade and publish them as a book. Around the time that I was working on this, an American nuclear-powered submarine, suspected of carrying nuclear arms, was scheduled to visit Yokosuka Port, which has a United States military base and was near my home in Kamakura. My middle son said he was going to a sit-in to oppose the visit. As a child, he suffered from severe asthma and had spent lengthy periods in treatment centers in Izu and Chiba to little effect. In fact, we had taken a gamble and moved from Tokyo to Kamakura because the doctor said there was 'a fifty-fifty chance' that it would cure him. Only the night before, he'd had another sleepless night due to an asthma attack. I prevented him from going. "You'll sit down, be dragged away by a police officer, sit down again, and so it will go on until you collapse or possibly even die. Please wait another ten years, then you'll be an adult and if you choose to take the anti-nuclear, peace campaigner path, I'll throw my full support behind you. Right now, you're better to focus your energies on getting well and do things more within your reach, such as donating some of your pocket money or signing petitions." At that, the usually mild-natured boy came up to me so close I thought our noses would touch; hands tightly fisted and tears rolling down his cheeks, he reproached me.

"You adults don't do a thing so we're obliged to act. You want peace, as a survivor of the bomb, yet do nothing. Life isn't easy, I know, but you could surely do something, like writing letters to the newspaper for instance."

That night, after he went to bed, I pondered over what I could do. I sat down at my desk and had just picked up the pencil I was using to transcribe the poems for my poetry collection when I suddenly had a flashback to the night of the bombing, the night I had spent with Iida under the golden inferno, showered in golden ashes. Dawn was beginning to break when I finally put my pencil down. Before going to bed, I made a boxed lunch for my son and, underneath the box, left a copy of the poem I had just finished composing. It began as follows:

Golden ashes raining down on our bodies.
Overhead, a roaring inferno.
In the thicket where we shelter
leaves crackle and pop,
our hair burns with a sizzle.
The depths of the night
awash in golden light.
City, engulfed in fire.
Cut off from life
yet passed over by death,
in a space beyond life and death.
The golden ashes will surely, eventually,
bury us...[78]

"Mum, I understand," my son said when he arrived home from school that day. He was sixteen years old, the same age as Iida had been on the day of the blast. Strangely, from that time onwards, the heavy lead-like weight that I had felt bearing

---

[78] Bun omits the latter half of this poem.

down on me for so long slowly began to lift. And, little by little, I was able to touch upon the subject of the atomic bombing.

In 1991, when I turned sixty, my eldest son said quietly, "Mother, I would like to see you live a life of your own, if only for five years." It made me stop and look back over my life. Raised according to traditional mores, I had lived with the belief that it was a virtue for a woman to devote her life to the family. I wanted to see what it was like to live for oneself. There was a mountain of things that I wanted to study, having unfortunately grown up in an era and environment that made studying impossible. I considered studying at the Open University[79] but that was not feasible, either financially[80] or time-wise. I chose in the end to study English, thinking that this would equip me to travel overseas alone. It occurred to me that regardless of one's nationality, ethnicity, religion, or culture, humans at heart are one and the same and share similar joys and sorrows. I wanted to meet people in South-East Asia, Central and South America, and African nations, compelled to live a hard life, and see for myself what life was like for them. It was with such extravagant thoughts that I began to study English. Those dreams suddenly became real when, at sixty-one, I travelled to Edinburgh, Scotland, for three month's study.

Prior to my departure, the husband of a friend of mine translated four of my poems on the bombing of Hiroshima and gave them to me to take to Edinburgh where I read them in class; faced with an actual survivor of the blast, the teacher and students received a big shock much as if they'd seen the bomb drop before their very eyes. Their reaction made me conscious of the fact that, even if I didn't speak the language, I could make a strong anti-nuclear statement simply by standing there in front of people. In an act of sheer impulsiveness, I had suddenly launched myself into this English language school, a

---

[79] The Open University of Japan is a distance education university founded in 1983 with the aim of providing open access to anyone that wishes to enrol. Hence there is no entrance examination.
Students study via radio and television and, more recently via internet.

[80] It required a costly antenna.

sixty-one-year-old housewife with virtually zero English skills! Though hard, the lessons were full of variety and included interesting field trips where we would be thrown into real life situations which made each and every day fun and satisfying. I was the oldest student in the class and my English language ability, limited, but I got by like everyone else. Nevertheless, when I read my diary from that time, I am reminded that my days were filled with many ups and downs.

After receiving some English training, I firstly visited Berlin. It was shortly after the German reunification. I had gone there out of the desire to stand, as a survivor of the atomic bomb, on the ruins of the Berlin Wall, another twentieth-century tragedy. I then toured around Europe alone. It is no exaggeration to say that my time studying in Edinburgh and travels abroad determined the future direction of my life.

Two years passed after my trip to Edinburgh. It was an immensely busy time: my mother had come to live with us after father died and we extended the house to accommodate her; I was diagnosed with suspected stomach cancer and underwent treatment; we took in Mei-Chen, a nineteen-year-old female tennis player from Taiwan, for a year. Throughout that time, I kept studying English though somewhat intermittently. Despite persevering, I saw no great improvement. Then the chance to study abroad arose again, this time in New Zealand after a club that I belonged to planned a two-week English language study tour there for senior citizens. Deeming two weeks too short, I decided to stay on after the end of the tour and continue my studies at another school. When I was preparing for the trip, my friend, Hiraoka Toyoko, gave me some valuable advice. She said that she had visited various places, including the foreign embassies, to spread the anti-nuclear message, and had found the New Zealand ambassador extremely supportive. "Please take this and go to meet the New Zealand ambassador," she urged, delivering me an English translation of the essay that I had written on the bombing of Hiroshima – she had sat up all night translating it. When I visited the New Zealand Embassy in Tokyo, the ambassador had already returned to New Zealand in preparation for his next posting. But he had left his secretary with another person's business card and instructions for me to meet that person while in New Zealand. The name on the card was Kate Dewes.[81]

New Zealand comprises two main islands, the North Island and South Island. While studying for two weeks at a school in Christchurch, a South Island city, I asked the Japanese administrator at the school, Hitomi, to take me to visit Kate Dewes. Kate is a cheerful, energetic mother of three who helped lead the campaign to challenge the legality of the threat or use of nuclear weapons at the World Court. This campaign resulted in the International Court of Justice in Hague in the Netherlands, issuing the advisory opinion in 1996 that nuclear weapons are 'contrary to international, and particularly humanitarian law'.

"Would you mind meeting my daughter?" Kate asked, after Hitomi had finished interpreting for me. "She's fourteen, the same age as you when you were exposed to the atomic bomb." Kate's daughter hugged me and burst into tears.

"When I learned at school about the bombing of Hiroshima," she said, "I couldn't sleep for nights on end." Standing behind her was a bearded man – Kate's partner, Robert Green.[82] He also hugged me, and said in muffled tones, "I'm British. I'm campaigning against nuclear weapons, but it's the first time that

---

[81] Kate Dewes is a long-standing New Zealand peace and anti-nuclear arms campaigner, and pioneer of the World Court Project as Bun explains. She has served on the International Peace Bureau, the International Steering Committee for the International Court of Justice and the UN Secretary General's Advisory Board on Disarmament Matters. She is Co-Director of the Disarmament and Security Centre based in Christchurch (see http://www.disarmsecure.org/people.php).

[82] Formerly a Commander of the British Royal Navy, Robert Green once flew around in Buccaneer carrier-borne nuclear strike aircraft and anti-submarine helicopters equipped with nuclear depth-bombs but is now Co-Director of the Disarmament and Security Centre, and the author of a number of books on the issue of nuclear deterrence, including *Security Without Nuclear Deterrence* (also available in Japanese under the title 核抑止なき安全保障へ; 2010). He has served as Chair of the UK branch of the World Court Project (WCP) and as a member of the WCP International Steering Committee.

I've ever met a survivor from Hiroshima," or at least that's what it sounded like to me with my limited English. The two hugged me, tearfully. Once again, I felt a strong sense of what it meant to be a survivor of the atomic blast, and was reminded that it didn't matter whether I could speak the same language, my mere presence was enough to convey the anti-nuclear message.

In New Zealand, nature and people's hearts are kind. In the past, people went out on yachts to prevent a United States nuclear-powered submarine from entering New Zealand ports. There are no nuclear power plants in New Zealand and there is overwhelming public support for the nation's anti-nuclear stance.[83] Once, I went on a short trip with a day pack slung over my shoulder and happened to sit next to a young sixteen or seventeen-year-old girl on the intercity bus. When, in broken English, I praised New Zealand's nuclear free policy, she replied, "Thanks. I'm proud of it too but it resulted in not only the United States[84] but also England and France,[85] imposing

---

[83] In 1984, when David Lange's Labour Party was swept into power following a snap election called by the then incumbent prime minister and leader of the National Party, Robert Muldoon, it immediately introduced a ban on nuclear weapons and nuclear-propelled warships. This was amidst a groundswell of opposition in New Zealand to nuclear weapons and nuclear tests. According to an opinion poll commissioned by the 1986 Defense Committee of Enquiry, 92 percent of all New Zealanders were opposed to nuclear weapons in New Zealand and wanted New Zealand to push for nuclear disarmament via the United Nations (see Dewes, Kate. "Legal Challenges to Nuclear Weapons from Aotearoa/New Zealand." *British Review of New Zealand Studies*, Number 12, 1999/2000). In 1987, the Lange-led government passed the New Zealand Nuclear Free Zone, Disarmament and Arms Control Act. This legislation remains in force today.

[84] In response to New Zealand's refusal in 1985 of a proposed visit by the Navy ship, USS Buchanan, the United States severed various intelligence and military ties with New Zealand, downgraded diplomatic and political exchanges and suspended its defense obligations under the ANZUS (Australia, New Zealand and United States of America) Security Treaty.

sanctions on us. That's hard on a small country like New Zealand. Still, we can't sell our souls down the road for the sake of money." I couldn't help speculating whether a young Japanese woman would be capable of holding such a conversation with a foreign tourist who happened to sit next to her. As the days passed and my experiences piled up, I fell in love with New Zealand.

My homestay for the over fifty-fivers' English study tour was with Trevor, an apiarist, and his wife Margaret. One day, Trevor said that he'd like me to speak to the Lions Club whose Board he was on. The seventy to eighty ladies and gentlemen gathered there were from a wealthy sector of society, a world apart from me. At the head table sat the Chair, a fine-looking gentleman, surrounded by four to five executives. Lined up down the table was a string of Union Jacks and stately looking flags emblazoned with the Lions' insignia. Hitomi, my interpreter, appeared even more nervous than me. The moment I finished talking, I was inundated with questions. "So did people know it was an atomic bomb that was dropped?" "Do you suffer from radiation sickness?" "Did the United States provide compensation?" "How did the Japanese government respond?" "How shameful that the American government didn't provide any compensation." "Why didn't the Japanese government protest?" And so on. Meanwhile a minor dispute arose among the participants; some criticized Japan's attack of

---

[85] New Zealand's relationship with France is complex. In 1973, amid growing opposition in New Zealand to nuclear testing in the Pacific, the New Zealand Prime Minister, Norman Kirk, sent a frigate to Mururoa (French Polynesia) to protest against French nuclear tests being conducted there. Then, in 1974, New Zealand took France to the World Court to challenge the legality of its nuclear tests. Relations reached an all-time low in 1985 when Greenpeace's flagship, Rainbow Warrior was sunk with explosives by agents of the French Foreign Intelligence Agency (DGSE) while docked in Auckland Harbour (New Zealand). The explosions also killed a photographer. Two agents, a commander and captain, were subsequently arrested in New Zealand and sentenced to ten years in prison. In response, France threatened to block New Zealand access to European Economic Community markets and boycotted New Zealand exports to France.

Pearl Harbor, others countered by saying that Pearl Harbor and the atomic bomb were separate issues. The debate ended with everyone agreeing that, regardless, the dropping of the atomic bomb was an unadulterated crime.

What surprised me was that only a handful of the men at the meeting had been to war. They were from that generation where, had it been Japan, virtually all of them would have been drafted. It struck me that a deep-seated resentment toward the United States for using New Zealand youth after the end of the war as shields for their soldiers in the Korean and Vietnamese wars may have been behind their criticism of the United States. When I left Christchurch, and went to stay in Auckland in the North Island, I likewise heard criticism of the United States. A seventy-year-old man doing voluntary work at the city museum spoke thus: "One month after the atomic bombings, I was stationed at Yamaguchi (Iwakuni[86]) as part of the Occupation Forces. I was nineteen. We had been told that there would be no dangerous effects from the bomb, but it was the New Zealand and Australian soldiers who were sent west after arriving in Tokyo while the American soldiers headed north. Immediately following our arrival in Yamaguchi, we went into Hiroshima day after day. Twenty out of thirty-eight of my comrades died from secondary effects of radiation exposure after returning to New Zealand. The remaining twelve of us suffer from radiation-related illnesses and have been appealing to the New Zealand government to recognize us as atomic bomb victims but to no avail. I worry about the possibility of my children and grandchildren suffering effects." I visited the museum where he worked the following year only to be told that he had been off work for some time due to illness.

---

[86] Iwakuni is a coastal city roughly 35 kilometers southwest of, and a 45-minute local train ride to, Hiroshima. During WWII, the city was home to a Japanese military air base that was used for training and defence purposes. After the war, the base was occupied by various military forces, including those from Australia and New Zealand, before becoming a United States Marine Corps air base in 1952. The base is still there today, serving as a military base shared by the United States Marine Corps and the Japanese Maritime Self-Defense Corps.

Several years later, I met someone similar in Christchurch, a friend of Kate Dewes called Ian.[87] He was likewise stationed at Iwakuni and commuted daily to Hiroshima. The devastation in Hiroshima was horrific, far beyond one's imagination. No one would believe him when he spoke, on his return home, of the horrors he witnessed. Understood by no one, he lived a solitary existence thereafter, his memories of Hiroshima locked up inside him. "Having met you today, I finally feel lighter at heart. Now I can die in peace," he said, giving me a hug. I was deeply moved. Not long after I returned to Japan, I received news from Kate of his death.

New Zealand is like a second home to me, owing most especially to the couple, Yoshito Ishido and Susan Bouterey, who have taken me into their hearts like a member of their own family. Sharing similar fundamental views, we are friends who understand each other well. Susan teaches Japanese language and literature at the University of Canterbury. Speaking Japanese like it were her native tongue, she has translated my works into English and acts as an interpreter for me locally. Whenever she is interpreting, I feel I can talk about anything without worrying. Yoshito likewise used to lecture at the University of Canterbury but is currently busy running his own violin company, work that takes him all around the world. Their two sons, Jun and Yuuki, are both in Europe carving out musical careers. Jun composed a piano piece based on my Hiroshima poems[88] and performed it at one of his recitals in New Zealand. I hear that he still performs this piece. And it was at a public lecture that Yoshito and Susan organized for me that I met the 'people's writer', Elsie Locke,[89] who became my 'Peace Mother'. Yuuki was only a baby at the time and Susan interpreted for me after firstly breastfeeding him in the waiting room. After the lecture, a petite, elderly woman came toward

[87] Reverend Professor Ian Dixon (1912–2006) served as a chaplain with the New Zealand forces firstly in New Zealand and Italy, and then in Japan as part of the Allied Occupation forces.

[88] See 'Young Boy' on page 195.

[89] Elsie Locke (1912–2001) was a New Zealand writer, historian and leading figure in the women's rights and peace movements. She was the co-founder of the Campaign for Nuclear Disarmament in the 1950s.

me, her hand outstretched to shake mine. "I would very much like to speak with you," she announced. This was Elsie Locke.

The next day, I went with Susan to visit Elsie at her home. "You must tell your story. You must write about it. The atomic bomb is not simply Japan's issue. It concerns the future of the world and this planet. It is only through stitching together survivors' stories that we can learn about the atomic bombings. If people like you don't pass on your stories, the most important truths will sink into oblivion." The tiny woman's penetrating gaze bore right into me. I was filled with an overwhelming sense of duty as a survivor. Ever since then, for over a decade now, I have taken myself to New Zealand each year. Taking Susan's translations of four of my poems and an essay on my experiences of the A-bomb, I created a booklet that I have been distributing, like sowing seeds, while travelling around the world to promote the anti-nuclear message and campaign for peace.

On a number of occasions, I have also participated in Christchurch's Hiroshima-Nagasaki Day ceremony, hosted by the city and local people, and in which Elsie was a key figure.

The main purpose of Christchurch's ceremony is captured in Elsie's words, "On each anniversary of the first use of the atom bomb in war, people in Hiroshima float lanterns on their river[90] in memory of those who perished. The Avon[91] flows into the same ocean. We float our lanterns on our own river to share their sorrow, and to affirm that we will continue to work for the removal of all nuclear weapons from the earth, and to secure for all humanity, a peaceful future."[92] On the evening of Christchurch's fiftieth Lantern Ceremony, a recital was given of 'Kumikyoku Hiroshima' (Hiroshima Suite), a lieder based

---

[90] The Ōta River.

[91] The Avon River, also known by its Maori name, Ōtākaro, is a major river that flows through central Christchurch, meandering through various suburbs before eventually flowing into the Pacific Ocean.

[92] Elsie Locke's words are quoted verbatim here as opposed to Bun's slightly condensed version in the original Japanese.

on four of my Hiroshima poems put to music by composer Hidenori Ao.[93]

Every year, when I met Elsie she would enquire, "Are you telling people your story? Are you writing?" And again, when we parted, "You must tell people, you must write." In November 2000, Elsie was awarded a Peacebuilder Award by UNESCO for her 'services to peace'. The award ceremony, held at the Christchurch City Council, was a congenial event attended by family and friends. "Look Bun," Elsie said, her face lit up with pleasure, as she showed me the award certificate, and she called over the photographer to take a photograph of us together. When I embraced Elsie as we parted, she said, arms laden with flower bouquets, "You must tell people your story, you must write," adding with motherly concern, "take care of your health!" Elsie passed away the following year, on April the 8th, 2001. She was eighty-eight years old at the time of her passing. By then, I too was in my mid-seventies and losing my physical strength. When Elsie died, I considered giving up on going overseas alone. The following year, I went down to Elsie's tiny cottage near the banks of the beautiful Avon River. It was undergoing renovations in preparation for her granddaughter to live there and was empty and bare. In Elsie's study, her desk sat forlornly in its usual corner. I went over and was lightly stroking it when I happened to look up and see on the wall above, a single photograph of the two of us. It gave me a jolt. I could almost hear her saying, "Bun, you must tell people, you must write." Once again, I began to write and to travel the world.

Kate Dewes and Robert Green are also like family to me now. Kate calls me her 'Japanese mother' and has a room at the ready for me whenever I visit. Robert has continued to campaign for the elimination of nuclear weapons. His two books, *Fast Track to Zero Nuclear Weapons: The Middle Powers' Initiative* and *The Naked Nuclear Emperor: Debunking Nuclear Deterrence* have been translated by Umebayashi Hiromichi and published by Kōbunken.[94] Robert

---

[93] 青英権 (1929–2013)

[94] The Japanese titles are: 核兵器廃絶への新しい道:中堅国家構想 (1999) and 検証「核抑止論」:現代の「裸の王様」(2000).

continues to put his energy into writing while Kate attends workshops at the United Nations as an advisor to the UN Secretary General, Ban Ki-moon, on the issue of nuclear arms abolition.

**Bun with Kate Dewes**

I have many other wonderful friends in New Zealand, in addition to those named above.

And over the last decade or so, I have traveled around dozens of countries, including Canada, Germany, Holland, France, Sweden, and visited innumerable cities. In each of those countries I have been fortunate to meet some very special people. There's Tessa, for instance, a Scottish poet whom I met on my study tour to Edinburgh when I was sixty-one. We took a liking to each other and have developed a deep friendship. We keep close company during the annual International PEN Club Convention, which she attends as the Scotland PEN Club representative, and I always feel as though she's close at hand.

Then, there is Andas, a Swedish chap that I met on the intercity bus in Ireland. After he returned to Sweden, he apparently wrote the words, 'Don't forget Hiroshima of 1945!' on a placard and paraded it through the city streets. Surprised at the lack of interest in nuclear arms, especially among the youth, he translated the booklet of my atomic-bomb essay and poems into Swedish and handed it out at schools and in town. Many times has he invited me to Sweden and arranged for me to give talks while there. Eva, a leading figure in the International Physicians for the Prevention of Nuclear War association, helped Andas create the Swedish version of my booklet. Several years older than me, she leads a busy life attending meetings across Europe for the International Physicians association and doing other things such as learning how to use the computer for the first time in her eighties. We are much like sisters now; whenever I stay at her home, her friends come to visit and we have a splendid time. Every year, in the ancient town of Orebro where she lives, a Hiroshima Day Lantern Ceremony is held. Eva is the organizer of the event. There's a mysterious, enchanted air as, amid a live performance of classical music, people's handcrafted lanterns carry the spirits of the dead downstream. I must have gone to Sweden four or five times now; Eva works tirelessly for me while I'm there, interpreting my speeches at the Lantern Ceremony and assisting with my school talks.

Next, there's Edith, an Austrian resident in Nice, France. Eight years my senior, she's a poet and a doctor of philosophy. Her apartment is my accommodation in Nice; she always opts to sleep on the sofa, kindly giving up her bedroom for me. Her family home is in Vienna where she has organized a recital of my songs and for me to give some talks.

When she visited Japan, I took her on a guided tour around Hiroshima.

In 1995, when I attended the International PEN convention in Australia, the presiding Consul-General in Perth, Imamura Yoshihiro, introduced me to a journalist by the name of Norman who interviewed me. Ten years later, in 2010, Norman visited Japan in order to interview me again. The resulting article also appeared in Hong Kong's largest English language newspaper. When he came to Japan recently on a private visit, I showed him around Kamakura.

It was while I was on a trip around the South Island of New Zealand that I met Marty, an American Jew and three years my senior. Like me, he was travelling alone. His raspy voice, facial features, and deadpan humor reminded me exactly of the film director, Alfred Hitchcock. We continued our travels together, staying at youth hostels along the way.

After enjoying a week as travelling companions, the day came for me to depart for Christchurch. I went down to the dining room early in the morning to find him already there waiting for me. Looking unusually serious, he began to speak. "My family came to America seeking asylum during my grandfather's time. Until very recently, I was a teacher. Some of my pupils lost both parents at Auschwitz. But I don't hate the Germans, war is to blame." He saw me off to the bus stop through thick fog.

"I hope we can meet again," I said.

"The world is small!" I heard him reply as the bus picked up speed, leaving him behind.

I have been fortunate enough to have made many more precious friends all over the world but I will save those stories for another book and will touch instead on another memorable Hiroshima Day ceremony that I attended while overseas; it was in Kingston, Canada, in 2002. I was invited to the event by one of the coordinators, a middle-aged gentleman named Alex who is a pediatrician, university lecturer, and also an artist. Kingston's Hiroshima Day ceremony is organized around children. The program began with a speech from the Mayor of Kingston, then a message from the Mayor of Hiroshima after which I was introduced. A Kingston choir sang some songs, I gave a speech and recited some of my poems and finally there was to be the floating of the lanterns. The children created the lanterns while the adults' events were in progress, assembling the frames, and wrapping them with sheets of paper on which they had written messages and drawn pictures of the sun and trees, or of children from around the world linking hands and the like. How bright and bursting with hope their drawings and messages all were! As night began to fall, the adults' ceremony came to a close and the children gently floated their handmade lanterns on a pond. Kingston faces the United States from across Lake Ontario. I have a lasting impression of a group of young American men who had come to Kingston on holiday and, moved by the ceremony, approached me with questions.

I was in Canada for three weeks during which time I also visited Toronto and six other cities. In addition to Hiroshima Day ceremonies in Canada, Sweden and New Zealand, I have also participated in one in Finland and am considering going next to the ceremonies in Norway and Iceland.

What follows are some examples of questions that arose at talks that I gave at schools and community gatherings overseas, and my responses to those queries.

"Did your philosophy on life change as a result of the atomic bomb?" (New Zealand, seventeen-year-old youth)

"It was a painful experience but I was also able to witness how remarkable humans can be under the most extreme conditions." I regretted giving such a complicated response but the next day, I received the youth's written impressions of the talk: "I was greatly shocked and moved by your talk on the atomic bomb. What moved me most were your words about witnessing how amazing people could be under such extreme conditions. Those words have changed my philosophy on life. From now on, I will live my life in such a way that, like you Bun, I won't lose sight of that remarkable side of humans."

"What would you have done if you were President?" (Sweden, young university student, male)

"If I were President, I would have revealed everything about nuclear weapons to the world. That way, everyone would know how terrifying they are and we would never have been visited with the nuclear age."

"Do you hate Americans?" (Sweden, high school girl) This question comes up in every single country that I visit.

"No, Americans, Swedish, Japanese, we're all humans. I don't hate individual humans but I can't forgive those who dropped an atomic bomb on humans."

"Do you wish to take revenge?" (same student) "No, I don't think hatred or revenge will bring about peace, do you?"

"Then what would make you forgive America?" (same student)

192

"If America took the initiative to eliminate all of their nuclear weapons and campaign worldwide for the elimination of them, I may at that point forgive her."

(The moment I said that, it dawned on me how little I had in fact forgiven America.)

"Sixty-three years have passed since the bombing. Do you still seek an apology and compensation from America?" (France, junior high school student, female)

"The dropping of the atomic bomb is the greatest crime since the beginning of human history. Surely the United States has a moral responsibility to acknowledge their crime and apologize not only to the victims of the bomb but to all humankind?" I replied.

"Am I correct in assuming that the Japanese government rightly covers all the expenses for your overseas talks?" (Sweden, high school student)

"No, the overseas organizers cover my expenses during my visits. I am frugal and keep living costs down when traveling alone by staying at youth hostels and with friends." I have been told that, in Germany, the government has established a program whereby they send survivors of the Holocaust to give talks in countries across Europe but we have no such program in Japan.

"Didn't the government provide food, clothing, and housing to the survivors and rebuild the city?" The answer is no. At the meeting where I was asked this particular question, a wave of anger toward the Japanese government swept through the room.

I was particularly impressed with a group of university students in Sweden who were interested in knowing what the Japanese people, particularly young Japanese, think about the bombing."

When I was speaking with some young people in Finland, several American youths, who happened to be there at the time, all voiced their desire to hear more about the atomic bombing of Hiroshima. "Please tell us about it. We want to know the truth," they said, deeply earnest. There were so many things I wished to tell them but on that occasion there was no one to interpret for me. On many such occasions have I been frustrated by the language barrier.

On one occasion, at a high school in Australia, I was surprised by the children's frosty reception. Once I began to speak, however, their expressions gradually softened and some even cried. When the usual question time came around, the room was suddenly in an uproar. Later, Kelly, the interpreter, explained, "Bun, there's something I neglected to interpret. The children were greatly shocked by their encounter with you as they hadn't really known any Japanese people before that. When question time began, they all blurted out, 'The Japanese people are human too, just like us.'" Hearing this, I was all the more astounded. It was at an elite school in Perth, the capital of the State of Western Australia. I expect the pupils had grown up with stories from their parents and grandparents about the inhumane actions of the Japanese Army during the Second World War. "But Bun, just think, at home tonight, they'll be talking all about you. That's wonderful, isn't it? Thank you so much, Bun!" exclaimed Kelly, her eyes brimming with tears. She is a fan of Japan.

After a talk I gave at a university in France, a female student came running up to say, "I'm American. I'm so sorry!" A high school boy in Sweden once asked, "How do you say mother in Japanese?" "Okaasan," I replied whereupon he hugged me and exclaimed with tears in his eyes, "Oh my *okaasan*!" And so it goes on. These students all tell me how much I have moved them and given them the strength to live. But I was likewise moved by, and received strength from them, a strength that led to each new departure overseas. And they would all ask, "Where does all that energy bubble up from?" *What is it*, I wonder, *that gives me strength and keeps me alive?*

There is the expression 'in an instant'. We often use this expression but a true 'instant' is literally like a blink of an eye. A young five-year-old American boy insisted that he wanted to hear about what happened the moment the bomb was dropped. "One second? You mean one minute, right?" "No, one second. Julian, close your eyes and now open them. Look, the city has disappeared and I'm injured all over." He was lost for words. It's difficult to talk about the very instant when the atomic bomb fell. Perhaps the following poem will help readers imagine what it was like.

## Young Boy

Here on the outskirts of Hiroshima
In the military parade grounds overgrown with grasses
At a quarter past eight
A young boy
Has he come looking for insects
So early in the morning?
Suddenly
A flash of light strikes the boy
Turning him into a pillar of fire
Instantly reduced to charcoal
He falls to the scorching ground
Legs splayed, arms outstretched
Black, hollow eyes glaring up at the sky
Mouth gaping upwards in a silent scream
Is he calling out for his mother?
For his brothers, sisters, or friends?
Or screaming in agony?
Not a single tooth
Or fingernail even, remaining
Still the blazing inferno continues to burn
The charred remains of the young boy

# Fukushima

Eleventh of March, 2011 saw the Great East Japan Earthquake and Fukushima Nuclear Power Plant disaster. As a nuclear disaster, the Fukushima disaster was rated Level 7, the most serious on the International Nuclear Event scale and equivalent in scale to the 1986 Chernobyl Nuclear Disaster. Fukushima is now known worldwide.

Ever since the accident, people have been living in a state of anxiety amid a flood of information on nuclear energy, radiation, radioactive contamination, internal injuries from radiation, and the like. One can learn a great deal about such issues these days from the many books and talks given by experts. One such expert and physician I greatly admire is Hida Shuntarō. Twenty-eight years old and in Hiroshima at the time of the blast, he devoted himself to the treatment of the injured in the days and months that followed. Baffled by the inexplicable deaths of otherwise healthy people who had come to Hiroshima after the blast in search of family or to provide assistance, he started investigating the internal effects of radiation, and has continued this research ever since. Dr. Hida explains complex scientific matters in simple, layperson terms. At ninety-five, he is still remarkably active giving lectures, supporting survivors of the atomic bomb, and writing.

Even when operating normally, nuclear power plants continuously emit small amounts of radiation and produce radioactive waste, the disposal of which is an unresolved issue. Even so, the number of nuclear power plants worldwide continues to grow. Now, after the Fukushima Nuclear Power Plant disaster, we are faced with vast amounts of additional radioactive waste leaked at the time of, and subsequent to the accident, while mountains of contaminated sludge, water, and soil are piling up by the day as the decontamination operations continue. Yet to be addressed are issues relating to the impacts of the disaster on our forests, mountains, and animal life. What's more, since it remains unclear how to deal with the damaged reactors and clean up after the accident, the entire nuclear facility appears destined to become a gigantic pile of waste in the not too distant future. Meanwhile, the country is dotted with nuclear power plants that are past the end of their life and will need to be decommissioned one by one. It's too big a problem for an ordinary citizen like me to grasp.

In what follows, I draw on my own personal experience to reflect on the situation.

Five days after the Fukushima Nuclear Power Plant accident, I left my home in Machida, Tokyo, and headed for Hiroshima, an unfinished manuscript in hand. I desired to write the final chapter of the manuscript with my feet firmly planted on Hiroshima soil, the nuclear ground zero. On the train, I felt emotionally crushed. *The damage is irreversible,* I thought. *It will affect not only Japan but the rest of the world and the future of our planet. What a heavy burden we're passing on to the next generation.* The following morning, I walked down to the Atomic Bomb Memorial Mound in Hiroshima Peace Memorial Park – a large mound of earth in which are entombed the ashes of around seventy thousand people whose identities have never been established (As an aside, between the sixth of August to the end of December 1945, one hundred and forty-thousand people are said to have died from effects of the blast which means that the Atomic Bomb Memorial Mound is the final resting place of half of those victims). I lingered at the Memorial Mound for some time communing with the silent voices of the dead. *If humans continue to behave like fools, all life on earth will perish,* I thought. *The only way to avert a nuclear disaster is to eliminate all nuclear weapons and nuclear energy from around the globe.*

In February 2010, an international convention on the effects of French nuclear testing was held in Algeria. I was to attend the convention as a representative of the survivors of the atomic bomb. The Japan contact for the convention was Mashimo Toshiki, a specialist on French nuclear testing. Kihara Shōji, a second-generation survivor from Hiroshima who has continued to campaign against nuclear power plants, was to accompany me. Unfortunately, just prior to departure, unforeseen circumstances forced me to cancel my trip but Mashimo, Kihara, and I have been close friends ever since.

During my stay in Hiroshima in 2011, I was interviewed by French journalists almost daily, their interest in me generated, no doubt, by the recent publication in French of my memoirs on the bombing of Hiroshima. Mr. Mashimo introduced the first group of journalists, having come to Hiroshima for the express purpose of interpreting for me. My plans to write the last chapter of my book while at ground zero stalled, caught up as I was with interviews, creating A-bomb survivor records, attending meetings, and the like. Nevertheless, I was anxious to do something and so I wrote an open letter to the people of Japan and around the globe. This was subsequently translated into English and circulated in Japan and overseas.

The questions the French journalists asked were remarkably straightforward. For example, "What do you think of the Fukushima disaster, as a victim of the atomic bomb?"

"Hiroshima and Fukushima will never be the same. Fukushima has suffered greatly. The disaster made it clear that humans don't have the capacity to clean up after a nuclear power plant accident. I hope that world leaders will look closely at the Fukushima disaster and learn from it."

"Do you consider nuclear weapons and nuclear energy one and the same?"

"Yes, they're the same."

"But nuclear weapons are military arms used to kill people while nuclear energy is a 'green energy' for peaceful purposes."

"The creation process is similar and they both emit radiation."

"Why, if nuclear power plants are so dreadful, do people build them?"

"For the profit, I imagine, of all those with ties to the nuclear energy industry."

This interview session had started around eight thirty in the evening. At midnight, it still wasn't over. Exhausted, I said, "I have three sons. I don't think I ever told them in so many words but there is one thing that I always hoped for as I raised them. That is that they not become the sort of people who sought wealth, glory, and power because that corrupts people. Today, it is not simply individuals who have become corrupted in this way but countries, especially first world countries." At that, the journalists threw their hands up in the air as if to say,

"Okay, you win!" and brought the interview to a close.

In 2009, when President Obama visited Tokyo, several A-bomb victims went to the American Embassy in Tokyo at the invitation of the NGO, Peace Boat.[95] It was around the time that President Obama made his 'Prague Declaration', creating quite a sensation in Japan.[96] Doubtful that I would be able to meet the President in person, I took along the little booklet containing English translations of a number of my poems and essay documenting my experience of the atomic bombing of Hiroshima. To this I attached a short letter that a friend had translated into English for me, and passed them to a member of the Embassy in the hope that the President might happen to glance over these while on his flight home. In the letter to the President, I wrote, "The United States of America has had a succession of presidents since the war but you are the very first to have touched, in your Prague declaration, on the matter of America's moral responsibility as the first country to use nuclear weapons on humans. I greatly admire you for that. I should, however, like to see your proposal for nuclear abolition encompass nuclear power plants as well as nuclear weapons. I fear that nuclear power plants will eventually destroy our planet Earth."

On one occasion, I received a visit from the photographer, Joe O'Donnell, whose photograph of a young boy standing in the burned-out ruins of Nagasaki after it was bombed swept him to fame. It must be over twenty years ago now as I was still

---

[95] A Japan-based organization that aims to promote peace, human rights, respect of the environment, and so forth, primarily via the world-wide voyages of its chartered passenger ship, 'Peace Boat'.

[96] In a public speech in Prague in 2009, Obama pledged to ratify the comprehensive nuclear test ban treaty, to convene a global summit for the elimination of nuclear stockpiles, and to demonstrate 'America's commitment to seek the peace and security of a world without nuclear weapons.' These efforts to advocate for a world without nuclear weapons helped earn him the 2009 Nobel Peace Prize.

living in Kamakura at the time. A friend, Hiraoka Toyoko, had introduced him to me and she interpreted on the occasion of his visit. O'Donnell landed in Japan immediately after the end of the war and entered Nagasaki as a photographer attached to the United States armed forces. He recounted how he had stood on the hill among the ruins of Urakami Cathedral in Nagasaki and, surveying the city below, whispered, "Oh dear God, what dreadful atrocity have we committed!" My mother was still alive at the time and spoke animatedly to him about her seven-year-old son (my younger brother, Hideo) dying when the atomic bomb was dropped on Hiroshima. Never before had I seen her so engrossed in relating her story about the bombing, and to think she was addressing a big, burly American she'd only just met! O'Donnell broke down in tears as he related his painful experiences in Nagasaki. There was no end of topics to talk about but the hours were ticking by. As we wrapped up our discussion of the bombings, I remarked, "It's not just a matter of nuclear bombs, there's also the nuclear power plants. They're a global issue."

These words of mine are captured in a tape-recording of our discussion.

The world witnessed the dawning of the nuclear age on the sixth of August, 1945. Even though atomic bombs were considered a threat after Hiroshima and Nagasaki, we humans pressed ahead with the further development of nuclear weapons. At the time of the 1954 Bikini Atoll nuclear tests – codenamed Operation Castle, these were a series of nuclear tests conducted by the United States of America on the two atolls, Bikini Atoll and Enewetok Atoll[97] – a Japanese fishing vessel was exposed to nuclear fallout in the first detonation, leading to the death of one of the crew.[98] The sea, atmosphere,

---

[97] Both atolls are in the Marshall Islands.

[98] The explosion of a 15 megaton hydrogen bomb on Bikini Atoll exposed the fishermen on the vessel, Daigo Fukuryū Maru (Lucky Dragon No. 5), to lethal doses of radiation. In addition to the one fatality, all of the other crew experienced acute radiation syndrome for some weeks afterwards before eventually recovering. Approximately 1,000 times more powerful than the bombs dropped on Hiroshima and Nagasaki, the bomb, codenamed 'Bravo', caused extensive radioactive contamination of

and land were also polluted by French nuclear tests conducted in the South Pacific (French Polynesia). Amidst all this testing, the New Zealand government declared to the United States, the largest holder of nuclear weapons, that all nuclear-armed or nuclear-powered ships would be barred entry to New Zealand ports,[99] and finally in 1987, passed anti-nuclear legislation, announcing loudly to the world the country's unequivocal anti-nuclear stance.[100]

Growth of the anti-nuclear movement worldwide helped bring about small reductions in the number of nuclear warheads. Nevertheless, the nuclear powers continue to keep nuclear weapons powerful enough to annihilate the world many times over. Additionally, despite a succession of nuclear power plant disasters – Three Mile Island, Chernobyl, and then Fukushima – more and more nuclear power plants are being constructed around the globe. Japan experienced the atomic bombing of Hiroshima and Nagasaki and yet we have crowded our small country with nuclear power plants. What's more, following the Fukushima power plant disaster, the government and nuclear energy companies are looking at exporting nuclear energy technology overseas. I even hear that there are some who desire for Japan to hold nuclear weapons. It's disgraceful!

As I recall, it was forty or so years ago that I went on a guided tour of the nuclear power plant at Tōkaimura.[101] The moment I stepped inside the gate, I felt a strong repulsion akin to fear, and the sight of the well-tended pines and immaculate,

---

surrounding islands, affecting the health of their inhabitants, including US servicemen stationed there, and rendering the atoll uninhabitable.

[99] 1984.

[100] The nation state of New Zealand is located in the south-west Pacific Ocean. For details of the legislation see: http://www.legislation.govt.nz/act/public/1987/0086/latest/DLM11 5116.html

[101] Tōkaimura is a small coastal town in Ibaraki Prefecture some 120 kilometers northeast of Tokyo. It is the site of Japan's Atomic Energy Research Institute, established in 1956, and of the country's first commercial nuclear power plant, built in the early 1960s and generating power from 1966 until its decommission in 1998.

clean-swept garden, as we were ushered inside, struck me as odd. We were eventually led to a large, glass-walled computer room which we were able to look into through the glass. Once again, I was struck by the cleanliness of the facility; not a speck of dust was to be seen anywhere.

Though I knew very little about nuclear energy at the time, it frightened me to think that they had to be so fastidious when operating the plant. There were three storehouses in the grounds. "What do you keep in the storehouses?" I asked.

"They're for low-level contaminated waste."

"Are we able to see inside?" After advising that two of the storehouses were already full, they opened the third to show me inside. It was already stacked half full with drums. *Our small country will soon be overrun with these drums,* I thought as I continued asking questions. "Where do you keep the highly-contaminated waste?"

"We pack it into ultra-strong glass containers, case them in metal and deposit them at the bottom of the sea." I swallowed my next thoughts which were, *What happens if the sea water rusts the metal casing? And can they withstand the regular earthquakes we have here in Japan?* We were taken down to the seashore. A torrent of water was pouring out from the plant into the sea. *This has to be contaminated water*, I thought. For lunch, we were given local seafood from Oarai but I could not bring myself to try even a single morsel of the large assortment of fresh sashimi on the lunch platter.

Following the Fukushima disaster, my worst fears are rapidly being realized in Japan. Besides the regular contaminated waste, additional amounts of contaminated water and other wastes are being discharged from the Fukushima nuclear facility as a result of the accident, and these are growing by the day. And then there's the damaged reactors to deal with. These are serious problems that will continue to affect our entire planet into the future. There is also the weighty issue of residual radiation and its effect on people's internal organs. My immediate family, relations, friends, and I have suffered from all manner of illnesses throughout the last sixty-seven years and not merely in the days immediately following the blast. Our exposure to the atomic bomb seems the only plausible explanation for all of these illnesses. Figures from the

Chernobyl accident clearly reveal damage to the internal organs to be a long-term effect of exposure to radiation.

With our atomic bombs and nuclear energy, we continue to pollute the atmosphere, sea, and land, causing profound damage to our planet that future generations will inherit.

Following the 2011 Fukushima disaster, there are moves to review our dependence on nuclear energy and advances are being made in the generation of solar, wind, and thermal energy, as well as energy from natural gas. I am not entirely supportive of these moves, however, as they result in significant destruction of the natural environment. In Japan, solar panels are being laid on former industrial and agricultural land. Will not the land underneath be ruined? Oil will eventually dry up. And what about the 'shale gas' currently in the spotlight?[102] Will we not end up destroying the very earth beneath our feet? Indeed, I suspect that the many earthquakes and tsunami that have been occurring in recent years around the Asia Pacific region are the result of the atomic and hydrogen bomb experiments conducted in the South Pacific. Given also the many other problems around the globe, surely it is time that humans, as merely one form of life on this forever-changing planet, learned to live in harmony with nature.

At the time of my exposure to the atomic bomb, I was a sensitive young woman. Survivors crawled along the ground with serious injuries, and lived off weeds and rain water to survive. We received no medical treatment or any support whatsoever from the government. All the time I wondered, *Why are we faced with this situation?* In the process of growing up, this query gradually grew into a vision for the future, a vision of a world made up of 'global citizens'. My overseas travels strengthened my belief in global citizenship and the conviction that we don't need any superpowers, or all-powerful leaders. My hope is that the spirit of Japan's 'Peace Constitution'[103] will cross the oceans and spread to other shores around the globe.

---

[102] Gas is removed from shale rock by a process known as 'fracking'.

[103] The three key pillars of Japan's Constitution are the notion that sovereignty lies in the people, respect of human rights, and the

# Appeal from Hiroshima

People of Japan and around the globe, I am a survivor of the atomic bombing of Hiroshima. I live in Tokyo and am currently in my eighties. On the eleventh of March 2011, the Great East Japan Earthquake struck, triggering the Fukushima Nuclear Power Plant disaster. At the time, I was in the midst of writing about my personal experiences of the atomic blast, and the lives of the people in Hiroshima before and after the bomb was dropped some sixty-six years earlier. I had completed most of the manuscript but the Fukushima disaster pained me greatly and I felt heavy at heart. I decided to return to my hometown Hiroshima to write the final chapter of my book from the vantage point of the nuclear ground zero. Arriving in the late evening, no sooner had I stepped from the train onto Hiroshima soil than I felt a heavy weight settle on my shoulders. For a moment I was unable to proceed.

Whenever I return home, I head straight down to the cenotaph in the Peace Memorial Park to commune with the souls of departed family members, friends, acquaintances, and the many other people who perished in the unimaginable horrors on the day of the blast. On this occasion, however, rather than offer up prayers to the departed, I made some requests. "Please help me stay alive a while longer. Please give me strength. Please guide me and show me the way forward."

On that fateful day when the atomic bomb was dropped, I was approximately one-and-a-half kilometers from the hypocenter. I suffered serious injuries that took me to the brink of death but I managed to survive after three people came to my rescue. Following the blast, I lived with my family in a tiny hut

---

renunciation of war and the threat or use of force as means of settling international disputes.

on the city's scorched fields. While there, I suffered from acute radiation symptoms, including high fevers, nose-bleeds and bleeding gums, severe diarrhea, nausea, purpuric rashes, and hair loss. Miraculously, I once again survived. From that time on, however, I have come down with one illness after another, and there hasn't been a single day when I have felt completely well.

An affliction that I found particularly painful was the so-called atomic bomb *burabura-byō* with its symptoms of extreme lethargy. Many times I pleaded with the doctor, "Please, just for a day, or an hour even, give me a body that feels fresh and light." And at night, before I went to bed, I used to pray that I wouldn't wake next morning. These afflictions were all the result of internal exposure to radiation. When radioactive matter is ingested via contaminated food, water, or air, it continues to emit radiation causing endless damage to the body's cells and genes in a process that continues till the day one dies. Only recently did I learn when visiting Hiroshima that cesium,[104] a term that has finally made its way into the media, damages the muscles and is the cause of atomic bomb *burabura-byō*. All those who were caught in the 'black rain'[105] on the day of the blast, or came to Hiroshima in search of

---

[104] Also known as caesium. Although Cesium (Cs) is a naturally occurring element, the form of cesium produced during the operation of nuclear power plants or the explosion of nuclear weapons (cesium-137), is radioactive, has a long half-life and is toxic. Since cesium has similar chemical properties to potassium in the body, it can confuse the body, on ingestion, into replacing its potassium with cesium which in turn can lead to various acute illnesses such as hypokalemia, a symptom of which is extreme lethargy.

[105] Radioactive rain that fell following the atomic bombing of Hiroshima. Containing mud and dust stirred up from the explosion and soot from the ensuing fires, the rain left sticky black marks wherever it fell, be it on people, houses, or other objects – hence the name, 'black rain'. The rain contaminated water wells and killed fish in rivers and ponds in areas where it fell, an area extending at least twenty-nine kilometers by fifteen kilometers inland, according to an early post-blast survey (cf. 'The Spirit of Hiroshima', Hiroshima Peace Memorial Museum, 1999).

people or to assist the relief efforts in the aftermath, as well as those exposed to radiation from nuclear tests and nuclear power plant accidents, suffer from internal radiation exposure. In the past, the effects of internal exposure to radiation were kept secret from the public. With the Fukushima Nuclear Power Plant disaster, the expression 'internal radiation exposure' finally came out into the open but without any accompanying details explaining what it actually entails – no doubt because this would render the government's nuclear energy agenda untenable.

For a time, nuclear energy was made much of as 'green energy' and 'dream energy', but after the nuclear power plant accidents at Chernobyl and Three Mile Island, the rhetoric was toned down. Nevertheless, in recent years, countries all around the globe have been racing to create nuclear power plants in what some refer to as a nuclear energy renaissance. Noting this trend, I was sounding the warning bells, convinced that another nuclear power plant disaster was inevitable somewhere in the not-too-distant future. That disaster has now happened, right here in Japan. Every second, high-level radioactive material is being leaked from the beleaguered Fukushima facility. There are no firm measures for putting a stop to this, nor is there any end to the crisis in sight. Our small, earthquake-prone country is home to more than fifty nuclear power plants. Many are situated in regions with declining populations[106] and lie directly above seismically active tectonic plates.

Fukushima Daiichi (No. 1) Nuclear Power Plant, the site of the current disaster, has six reactors. After a series of explosions, they are in a critical condition. Fukushima Daini (No. 2) Nuclear Power Plant's four reactors likewise suffered damage. On the fifteenth of March, 2011, only days after the Great East Japan Earthquake, Shizuoka was hit by a big earthquake. A major earthquake is predicted to hit Suruga Bay in the Tōkai region[107] along the Pacific coast in the first half of

---

[106] This is no doubt due to the unspoken fear of a nuclear disaster but can also be seen as a reflection of discriminatory practices toward outlying areas in Japan.

[107] Suruga Bay is in Shizuoka Prefecture on the east coast of Japan, some 140 kilometers or so south of Tokyo. It falls within the Tōkai

the twenty-first century. Located in this region is the large-scale nuclear facility, Hamaoka Nuclear Power Plant. The earthquake-prone Japan Sea coastline is likewise dotted with nuclear power plants and home to Japan's 'Nuclear Ginza' located in Fukui Prefecture.

Fellow countrymen and women, do you find it acceptable that our country, Japan, a victim of the atomic bomb, should now be the cause of radioactive fallout? There is no time to waste. Let us call for the closure of all nuclear power plants currently in operation. People around the globe, please give us your support. Let us unite and demand not only a halt to the construction of additional nuclear power plants, but also the closure and decommissioning of all those in operation.

As an A-bomb survivor, I have long campaigned against nuclear weapons and energy at home and abroad. That is because I fear that there will come a day when, not only the atomic and hydrogen bombs but nuclear energy too will decimate life on earth. Even during routine operation, nuclear power plants constantly emit small amounts of radioactive material into the environment, polluting the sea, atmosphere, and land. The danger of these small amounts of radiation has, like other issues, been kept concealed from the public.

Humans are not the only life form on earth. Is it not sheer arrogance for us humans to sacrifice other forms of life for our own benefit? Surely we should use our wisdom to create ways to live in harmony with nature. In terms of the long history of humankind, we in the twentieth and twenty-first centuries are here for but a moment in time; for but a fleeting moment are we Earth's stewards as we take up the baton from our forebears to then pass on to future generations.

People exposed to radiation as a result of the Fukushima disaster will suffer the effects for the rest of their lives just like A-bomb survivors such as myself and all those affected by nuclear tests and previous nuclear power plant accidents. Every day we see reports in the media on the tough living conditions borne by people housed in the evacuation centers. I am moved by the plight of innocent babies and children caught up in this

---

region which in the past has suffered major earthquakes at regular 100–150-year intervals with the last one occurring in 1854.

tragedy but the sight of their irrepressible vitality in the midst of such hardship also gives me hope. Radiation is particularly harmful to children and their growth. Yet the government and power companies are pressing on regardless with their agenda to build another ten or so nuclear plants in this small, earthquake-prone country of Japan.

Radiation knows no borders. People of the world, let us join hands and take a stand against nuclear energy so that we may save our children who are the key to the future.

Atomic-bomb survivor, Hashizume Bun

29 March 2011

# My Health Since the Blast

1945: On the sixth of August, an atomic bomb is dropped on Hiroshima. Approximately 1.5 kilometers from the hypocenter, I suffer severe injuries. I am fourteen years old. Early the following morning, on the seventh of August, I suffer a severe attack of diarrhea – a condition that plagues me for many years afterwards. Several days later, I experience acute radiation poisoning symptoms that include, in addition to the dysentery, high fever, nosebleeds and bleeding gums, purpuric rashes, hair loss, aching all over. I don't recall how long these symptoms continued but every day was a painful struggle and I was conscious that death was never far away.

1947: During a regular medical check-up at work, I am diagnosed with cataracts and astigmatism. Additionally, every year for several years after the blast, I am in and out of hospital in summer due to high fevers and acute diarrhea. I suffer also at this time from herpes. My lips end up scabby all over after becoming inflamed and breaking out in sores; it is difficult to eat or sleep well at night. This condition continues to afflict me until I am twenty-four. I go with my mother to every single hospital and medical center in town but they are unable to find the cause and advise us that there is no cure. At twenty-four, I am told that I might have Erythematodes, a newly discovered disease being researched at the time at the Tokyo Telecommunications Bureau Hospital.[108] Antibiotic cortisone (steroids) help alleviate the symptoms but I continue into my sixties to make regular visits to the hospital for treatment of this

---

[108] Also known as systemic Lupus Erythematodosus. An autoimmune disease whereby the body's immune system mistakenly attacks healthy tissue. It can affect the skin, joints, kidneys, brain, and other organs.

affliction. The Adrenocorticotropic hormone (ACTH) injection that I am given while in hospital causes a shock reaction that takes me to the brink of death.

1961: (Thirty years old). I marry.

1962: My first child is stillborn.

1964: I give birth to my oldest son. After the birth, I continue to bleed and am in a critical condition.

1967: (Thirty-six years old). I give birth to my middle son. It is a normal birth.

1970: I give birth to my third and youngest son in a normal delivery, despite talk of a Caesarian. Today, my three sons and four grandchildren are all healthy. If I were to question anything, it would be my middle son's asthma as a child.

1981: (Fifty years old). My gallbladder and appendix are removed. Afterwards, I suffer from severe internal bleeding requiring treatment and regular checkups with a gastro-camera for the next four or so years.

1996: (sixty-five years old). My cataracts are surgically removed. Shortly after, my eyesight deteriorates again and I undergo laser treatment involving the creation of thirty or so tiny laser burns or openings in each eye. I still suffer from the after-effects of this today, requiring me to make regular hospital visits for treatment. In addition, I also now suffer from dry eyes and glaucoma, a condition that attacks the eye's optic nerve and can lead to blindness.

2003: (seventy-two years old). I have a bad fall while on a trip to Norway to spread the anti-nuclear message. I am found to have smashed a vertebra in my upper spine and one in my lower lumbar. My bone density drops to around half of what is considered normal. I continue to go to hospital, even now, for rehabilitation exercises and medication. To date, I have broken my ribs and collarbone more than ten times while going about normal daily activities. After the accident in Norway, old problems with diarrhea reoccur and continue for almost a year. My arms and legs break out in red lesions, early symptoms of sarcoidosis (an affliction that attacks the entire body). I am found to have enlarged ovaries, cancer being the suspected cause.

2004: A cancerous growth is removed from my large intestine. Ever since, I have undergone yearly colonoscopies.

Once again, I am diagnosed with the systemic inflammatory disease sarcoidosis. Currently, my only symptoms are lesions but I am told that if the disease spreads to my internal organs, I will need to be hospitalized and undergo steroid treatment in order to survive. Warned also that the disease can affect the eyes, I continue to have regular checkups with skin and eye specialists.

2005: I lose my sense of taste due, I am told, to an iron and zinc deficiency. This condition takes several years of hospital treatment before it is cured.

2008: I suffer from sudden loss of hearing in my left ear.

2009: (seventy-eight years old). Medication I am given for a colonoscopy damages the functioning of my kidneys and I suffer renal failure. This is now a chronic problem. They find pre-cancerous polyps in my colon.

2010: I undergo colon surgery to remove three polyps. I suffer from sudden loss of hearing in my right ear.

2011: I undergo surgery for conjunctivochalasis. I have a transient ischemia attack.[109]

2012: More polyps in my colon are surgically removed.

2013: I am afflicted with glaucoma.

2014: I am hospitalized with acute laryngitis. More polyps are found in my colon during a routine colonoscopy. These are being monitored.

Since the day of the blast, I have not had a single day of good health. Almost seventy years on, my legs still occasionally break out in purple lesions the size of a thumbprint, although there is no accompanying pain or itchiness and they usually disappear after several weeks. Other afflictions include, atomic bomb *burabura-byō* (acute fatigue), blood circulation problems, rheumatism, degeneration of the upper spine (degenerative cervical spondylosis), and osteoarthritis, osteoporosis, and UV radiation damage.

---

[109] A transient episode of neurologic dysfunction caused by a disruption of cerebral blood flow; often referred to as a mini-stroke.

# Afterword

Was I destined to become a victim of the atomic bomb at fourteen, during puberty, when one is so impressionable? A deep thinker as a child, I have felt and reflected on a myriad of matters since that fateful day of the blast and while surviving countless scrapes with death.

Due to war time, and then on account of the atomic bomb, I only received a limited school education. And it is fair to say that this merely consisted of the 'three Rs'; reading, writing and arithmetic. Everything I have learned beyond this has been self-taught and based on my own experiences. Of all my experiences in life, I believe it is the atomic-bombing that has made me an acutely 'thinking person'. The scenes of life and death that I witnessed in that melting pot of hell were on another plane far beyond our conception of war. *How could this be*? I asked myself and was thrown into deep contemplation on the reasons for such a horrific event and indeed, the meaning of life.

On the other hand, the atomic bombing was a defining moment in my life – an experience that has enabled me to survive to this day through many illnesses and hardships after my rescue from the brink of death. As I described in the main body of this book, it was in that nightmarish post-blast hell that I discovered how remarkable humans could be in the face of the most extreme conditions. I recall also, the exquisite feeling of delight at being alive that the sight of the sun aroused in me as I watched it set over the endless expanse of the atomic wasteland or when I gazed up at the myriad of stars shimmering in the night sky and radiating a soft light over our dark, unlit city of death. Such sights impressed upon me how tiny yet precious human life is, here for but a fleeting moment in the endless cycle of the natural universe. Perhaps owing to this awareness, I have found contentment in putting my trust in people and living a simple life.

For over a decade now, my life has involved going on solo trips overseas to promote peace and the elimination of nuclear arms and energy. If I include trips to international P.E.N. conventions, and those with friends, I have traveled to over fifty different countries and visited innumerable cities. I also participated in a round-the-world trip for A-bomb survivors, organized by the NGO Peace Boat. Looking at the world map, I have gone from one end of the world to the other, from New Zealand's Stewart Island near the South Pole to Norway's Tromsø near the North Pole. On these travels, I have seen and experienced first-hand the lives of many people in many different lands. Although I only managed to acquire a smattering of English after starting to learn the language at the age of sixty, I have nevertheless been able to use it to find my way around numerous cities and countries. Through heart-warming encounters with people, I have reached my own understanding of nature, the environment, culture, customs, national character, religion, politics, and many other aspects of life; reflecting on these matters has taken me another step forward.

I have been fortunate to meet some remarkable people, to have some rare encounters that have greatly enriched my travels and led me to visit the same countries time and again. I must have traveled to New Zealand on over ten occasions. When in 1994, I first visited New Zealand, I learned of the annual 'Hiroshima Day' ceremony – now called 'Hiroshima, Nagasaki Day' – held in Christchurch. I was deeply moved when I heard the purpose of the ceremony described as thus: "On each anniversary of the first use of the atom bomb in war, people in Hiroshima float lanterns on their river in memory of those who perished. The Avon flows into the same ocean. We float our lanterns on our own river to share their sorrow, and to affirm that we will continue to work for the removal of all nuclear weapons from the earth, and to secure for all humanity a peaceful future." The following year, in 1995, I participated in Christchurch's fiftieth anniversary commemoration event, including the floating of the lanterns, and have since attended on many occasions. The sea connects the world. And it was from the sea that human life was born.

Hiroshima, Nagasaki commemorations are held in a large number of cities throughout the world. Other commemorations that I have attended include those held in Sweden's Orebro, in Kingston, Canada, and Helsinki, Finland. What I have gained from these experiences is a globally shared vision of peaceful co-existence. Ever since that fateful day of the atomic blast when I was fourteen, I have wondered how we can create a better world. Peaceful co-existence is my present answer to that question as well as to the multitude of other pressing problems such as global warming and nuclear issues.

While I acknowledge that national borders are human-made, is it not the case that national character, culture, people's values, and the like are cultivated by the land and environment of a given country? If we truly hope for peaceful co-existence on earth, then surely the only way to realize this aim is for us to recognize such differences in national character, culture, and so forth, and build a future from the broad perspective of 'global citizens'. That should not be insurmountable for us. After all, families, communities, and nations are made up of individuals all with their distinct personalities. Are we not well past that era when we should be resorting to wars over differences in ideology, ethnicity, religion, national interests, or in retaliation? In particular, we need to understand that nuclear dependence will lead to the annihilation of the world.

I will continue to experience and reflect on many things. While in my twenties, I wrote haiku. My teacher invariably described my poems as having a 'certain beauty in their incompletion'. In my youth, I sometimes felt saddened by his evaluation. But as the years have piled up, I have grown to recognize the brilliance of those words 'beauty in incompletion'. Until the day I die, I wish to retain that freshness in conception.

Bun Hashizume

Hiroshima City immediately after the atomic bombing. Image taken by the US Army and kindly provided by Hiroshima Peace Memorial Museum. Visible on the right-hand side of the image is a white track like that Bun described staggering home along on the day after the bombing. In the distance can be seen Mt Aki-no-Kofuji on the small island of Ninoshima, also called 'Seto Fuji,' where Bun's father was told to search for his daughter.